THE SILENT SOUTH

PATTERSON SMITH REPRINT SERIES IN
CRIMINOLOGY, LAW ENFORCEMENT, AND SOCIAL PROBLEMS

A listing of publications in the SERIES *will be found at rear of volume*

G.W.Cable.

PUBLICATION NO. 57: PATTERSON SMITH REPRINT SERIES IN
CRIMINOLOGY, LAW ENFORCEMENT, AND SOCIAL PROBLEMS

THE SILENT SOUTH

Together with
THE FREEDMAN'S CASE IN EQUITY
THE CONVICT LEASE SYSTEM
THE APPENDIX TO THE 1889 EDITION
and
EIGHT UNCOLLECTED ESSAYS
ON PRISON AND ASYLUM REFORM

By GEORGE W. CABLE

With an Introductory Essay
GEORGE W. CABLE AS SOCIAL REFORMER
And Selected Bibliography
By ARLIN TURNER

Montclair, New Jersey
PATTERSON SMITH
1969

"The Silent South," "The Freedman's Case in Equity," "The Convict Lease System," and the "Appendix" are taken from the 1889 edition published by Charles Scribner's Sons, with whom special arrangement has been made for this reprinting.

The eight essays on prison and asylum reform were originally published in the New Orleans *Democrat* and *Times-Democrat* in 1881-82. They appear for the first time in book form in this edition.

The introductory material by Arlin Turner was prepared especially for this edition.

SBN 87585-057-X

Library of Congress Catalog Card Number: 69-14915

CONTENTS

viii CONTENTS

THE CONVICT LEASE SYSTEM
IN THE SOUTHERN STATES

APPENDIX TO THE 1889 EDITION

ESSAYS ON PRISON AND ASYLUM REFORM

GEORGE W. CABLE AS SOCIAL REFORMER

GEORGE W. CABLE
AS SOCIAL REFORMER

By Arlin Turner

AN ESSAY entitled "The Freedman's Case in
Equity," in *Century Magazine* for January, 1885,
charged that the former slaves did not receive justice in the courts and in other ways were denied
their full rights as citizens. The essay brought back
into public discussion questions that had been
largely in abeyance since the last Reconstruction
governments had withdrawn from the South eight
years earlier, and it thrust the author, George W.
Cable, into a campaign for Negro rights which during the following ten years would absorb much of
his thought and effort. Later in 1885 Cable collected this essay with two others into a book, *The
Silent South,* a comprehensive account of the social problems then dominant in the South, and one
of the most perceptive analyses which have been
published on the race issue in America.

When the essay appeared, Cable was traveling
with Mark Twain on a joint reading tour which set

the high mark for such undertakings. As they filled
halls during four months in the United States and
Canada, Cable held his own with his partner and
at times was in greater favor with the audiences.
His novel *Dr. Sevier* had just been published. Earlier he had written a collection of stories, *Old
Creole Days* (1879), a novel, *The Grandissimes*
(1880), a novelette, *Madame Delphine* (1881), and
a history, *The Creoles of Louisiana* (1883). On the
pages of these books he had delineated the character, speech, and culture of Creole New Orleans,
which had come to be identified as his literary province. His works had won critical acclaim, moreover, in both England and America, and he was
commonly ranked among the major novelists of his
time.

Cable was aware that the energy he spent in reform efforts reduced his literary output at a time
when he had great inducements to push ahead
writing fiction. He was aware also that in cham-
pioning Negro rights he was alienating many of
his friends and supporters, and in fact was inviting
such ringing denunciation and even crude vilifica-
tion that some of his friends had fears for his
safety. The "great sore question," as he called it,
commanded his first efforts, nevertheless, until past
1890, when he saw state laws enacted which fixed
the Negroes in a restricted status, presumably to
remain, and he saw his publishers — and the North

generally — eager to drop the wearisome subject and leave the Southern states to solve the race problem in their own way.

George Washington Cable (1844-1925) was not new in 1885 to social reform. He had earlier organized and led citizens of his native New Orleans in a highly successful campaign for reform of prisons and asylums. A logical next step was an attack on the convict lease system which prevailed in the Southern states. Again he won wide public approval, but only partial success, since powerful economic and political forces defended the system. An equally logical next step brought him to champion, first, the cause of justice for ex-slaves in the courts and, beyond that, the extension of full civil rights to Negroes.

Cable's failure in the Southern debate was a temporary failure. When the problem was taken up again, more than half a century later, the movement was inevitably in the direction he had pointed. In lectures, essays, and fiction he dealt with a surprisingly full range of the issues which would confront later generations. He enunciated principles which have echoed through later discussion of civil rights; and he had reached an understanding of social, political, and moral implications in the questions under debate which his successors have found surprisingly acute.

Nothing in Cable's appearance or his background seemed to fit him for leading campaigns in social reform or for standing alone against public wrath. Five feet two inches tall and normally weighing less than a hundred pounds, he dropped out of high school to begin work before graduating. His father (also named George Washington) had prospered in the era of plunging expansion in New Orleans and on the lower Mississippi River and had owned slaves, but at his death in 1859 he had left nothing to support his widow and three children. As a clerk in New Orleans, a Confederate cavalryman, a bookkeeper and newspaper reporter after the war, the future novelist and reformer showed no marked differences from his associates, except for an uncommon devotion to self-education and a habit of reducing issues to root questions of morality and justice. In a column of miscellaneous comment written for a New Orleans newspaper, the *Picayune,* in 1871 and 1872, he reflected an alertness to affairs about him; in a series of historical sketches printed later in the same paper on "The Churches and Charities of New Orleans" he revealed an interest in local history and a special awareness of the present as an outgrowth of the past.

These early writings, along with his work in the programs of his Presbyterian Church, bear clear evidence that by temperament and interest Cable was a reformer. He and his wife joined in an almost formal dedication to humanitarian endeavors, such as his work in the Sunday School which he organized and led in its programs of social improvement for the dispossessed of the city. In 1872 he welcomed the occasion to bring his bent for reform and his gifted pen together in writing newspaper editorials attacking the Louisiana Lottery Company, which had such wealth and such political power that it remained impregnable until the enactment of Federal laws twenty years later. This effort was commissioned by a local newspaper and had wide backing in the city. In his next attempt at reform, Cable was without such backing.

In an essay entitled "My Politics," which he left unpublished,[1] Cable told how his thoughts on slavery had progressed. Early unquestioning acceptance of the institution gave way to doubts soon after the war as he tested in his own mind its constitutional and biblical defenses. Later he became convinced that slavery had been a moral wrong which left its marks on both slaves and slave-owners, and that comparable wrong and comparable evil were produced in the post-war South by denial of rights to the former slaves. During the Reconstruction era children of both races attended school together in some of the New Orleans schools, including the Girl's High School in the building

[1]Published in *The Negro Question: A Selection of Writings on Civil Rights in the South by George W. Cable,* ed. Arlin Turner (New York, 1958, 1968), pp. 1-25.

known as the Haunted House in Royal Street. In
1875, a white mob went to the building and expelled
all pupils not of pure blood. Cable chose the *Bulletin*, the local newspaper most vociferously opposed to the mixed schools, and wrote the editor a
letter signed "A Southern White Man," decrying
the purpose and the means of the mob action. The
editor published his letter on September 26 but
accompanied it with a rejoinder of equal length,
and he declined to publish a second letter Cable
submitted.[2]

Cable laid the rejected letter away with a note
saying he thought that after ten years his views
would be generally accepted in the South. The editor's rebuff was clear evidence that the question
Cable had raised could not yet be discussed in the
public press — the Radical Party and the Democratic Party were still locked in a struggle for control, which more than once broke out in armed con-
flict in the streets. In two of his early stories, however, "Belles Demoiselles Plantation" and "'Tite
Poulette," both published in 1874, Cable touched
on the problem of race.

When he next took up the cause of reform
openly, Cable had generous public support. In 1881
he served as secretary of a local grand jury. After
he had written the report[3] and the jury had been

[2]The published and the unpublished letters are included in
The Negro Question, pp. 26-33.
[3]Printed on pages 217-227 of this edition.

dismissed, he was determined that the findings and the recommendations should not suffer the usual fate of being ignored and forgotten, while the prisons and asylums continued in a state which he once said "would bring the blush to a murderer's cheek." The program he brought forward was a model in minute planning, management of the persons and agencies required, and vigorous execution. Its success went beyond all expectations and he was praised accordingly.

The moving force in the program was to be public opinion, mobilized by Cable and a few other dedicated workers, inspired by the enlistment of prominent citizens in the undertaking, and furnished with information on local conditions and on what might be learned from progressive institutions elsewhere. An avenue for publicity was assured when a daily newspaper, the *Times-Democrat*, adopted Cable's program as its own. The editor, E. A. Burke, wrote on December 16, 1881, soliciting the benefit of Cable's "researches, investigations, and plans connected [with] the reform of the public correctional and penal institutions and charities of our city and State, and also in the matter of the suppression of crime." He contracted to publish a series of articles Cable would write, and in effect turned his paper, in its news-gathering as well as its editorial departments, into an agent for local reform. On a trip east in June, while a member of the grand jury, Cable had been commissioned by the mayor of New Orleans, Joseph A. Shakespeare, to visit comparable institutions in Boston, Concord, and Hartford in search of information and ideas for use locally.

Cable's first direct move was to call in the help of three friends and draft an ordinance for adoption by the city council in November. The ordinance provided for a fifteen-member, non-political, self-perpetuating Board of Prison and Asylum Aid Commissioners, charged with inspecting each of twelve local institutions quarterly and proposing action to bring improvement. Aware that he must win the support of practical businessmen, Cable explained that the Board would have for these institutions the same responsibility a board of directors has for a private stock company. He had helped assure the adoption of the ordinance by furnishing the names of half a dozen friends and business acquaintances willing to serve on the commission. The Rev. Hugh Miller Thompson, pastor of Trinity Episcopal Church, became chairman, and the other members were prominent business and professional men. The *Times-Democrat* published on Christmas Day two articles by Cable recounting the steps already taken and the plans for the future. Additional articles appeared at intervals of two weeks, making a total of seven.[4] Burke wrote

[4]Printed on pages 228-271 of this edition.

an editoral to accompany each article, endorsing Cable's position and declaring that his paper would support the program until, as he wrote on February 12, 1882, "the monstrous wrongs that Mr. Cable has demonstrated are corrected and set right."

On January 2, 1882, the Board of Prison and Asylum Commissioners met and initiated the next step in the sequence Cable had planned: the formation of a constituency for the Board, a Prisons and Asylums Aid Association, to have as members all who wanted to see the institutions improved and who would receive such information on the subject as the Board would provide them. The Association would meet once a year, like the stockholders of a business corporation, and would serve mainly to link the Board of Commissioners and the public at large, to assist in spreading information, and especially to give reform efforts such a wide political base in the community that they could not be ignored or opposed with impunity. The membership of the Association had reached 250 before the organizational meeting was held on March 7. W. R. Lyman, president of the Crescent Insurance Company, became president; the other officers — and indeed a large proportion of the members — were well known.

Taking the office of secretary of the Board of Commissioners, without pay, and with a paid assistant, Cable lost no time in setting his program in motion. His grand-jury report the preceding June had made comparisons with institutions he had visited in the East. He set out now to assemble a library of official reports and other documents from the parishes of Louisiana, other states, and several foreign countries. Both the Board of Commissioners and the Association worked through committees, collecting information for dissemination through the press and other means, and submitting proposals through the Board of Commissioners, which met each month, for action by the city and the state governments.

Current events, purposefully reported in the press, served to smooth the way for several of the proposals. A scandal at the city insane asylum, where the bathing and other care of female inmates was done by male attendants, made it easier to persuade the director of the asylum to appoint female attendants and thus, the director said, "to please chronic fault-finders." The recommendation that matrons be hired for service in the parish prison and the precinct stations was supported by the press report of a woman who had been required to undress for searching by the two officers who had arrested her. A description of a boys' orphanage located in a swamp led to its removal to a less infectious location. Cable's articles, supplemented by newspaper reports and editorials, stirred and directed the public so effectively that three major reforms were achieved: the state legislature enlarged the facilities at the state asylum in Jackson enough for the New Orleans asylum to be closed and its inmates to be transferred to the state institution; a fund of $200,000 was provided for a new parish prison building in New Orleans; and an ordinance was passed by the city council setting up detailed regulations for prison management.

Cable answered all cries that the reforms would cost too much by invoking moral considerations. Society had produced the inmates of the institutions, the criminal and the insane, and hence could not shirk the burden of caring for them.

It was a conviction of Cable's that informing members of society that injustice or inhumanity existed among them and appealing to their moral and social consicence would bring about reform. This conviction was borne out, he believed, by the achievements of the Prisons and Asylums Aid Association. It was his habit to note practical considerations, but he did not hesitate to declare that nothing can be practical which is not right. To him, moral and humanitarian considerations took precedence, but he was pleased if he could argue also, as he could in urging prison and asylum reform, that he was supported by practical requirements for public well-being. Public funds spent to protect society from criminals (and also funds spent on public education) were a paying investment;

funds spent for the care and rehabilitation of the criminal and the insane could be credited to both wise civic management and humanitarian action. These were the considerations that held Cable engrossed in reform programs in his native city and state; the same considerations prompted him to the next stage of his career as reformer. One step, he said, led to another.

Through the reports of the state penitentiaries Cable discovered an area in which the injustice and inhumanity far exceeded, at least in scope, anything he had found in New Orleans. He learned about the contracts under which each of the Southern states leased its convicts as a labor force in private undertakings. The system invited his attack at several points: the attempt to make prisons financially self-supporting; the exploitation of the convicts for private gain; the consequent lack of care, extending from food and medical care to educational and religious attention; the lack of adequate records; the large number of escapes; the short life-span in the penitentiaries; and the overall brutality of the system. It was this sorry story, buttressed by statistics from the separate states and pitched in a tone of moral condemnation, that Cable told in addressing the National Conference of Charities and Correction at Louisville, September 26, 1883. Entitled "The Convict Lease System in the Southern States," this address appeared the next February in *Century Magazine*, and was included in 1885 with two other essays in *The Silent South*. It brought Cable prominently onto the national scene and won praise from all except a few apologists for the lease system.

Studying the penitentiary reports had brought Cable two conclusions more disturbing than any he had reached previously. Some of the convicts were serving inordinately long sentences (under conditions which made any sentence beyond a few years in effect a life sentence), and the proportion of Negroes among the convicts was far greater than might be expected, even after allowance for the extenuations usually offered. The address written for delivery at Louisville originally contained a section on these findings, but Cable deleted it, not wanting to lessen the force of his attack on the lease system and still hesitant to take a position on the race question which he knew would drive away many who supported his other reform efforts. But since writing letters to the editor of the *Bulletin* in 1875, he had not been satisfied to remain quiet on a social and moral wrong which he believed overshadowed all others.

In commencement addresses at the University of Mississippi in 1882 and at Tulane University the next year, he had skirted the issue so closely as barely to avoid stirring the ire of politicians and newspaper editors. He called slavery "an error as

wide as the nation," and he lamented that because
of its "peculiar institution" the South had stepped
aside from the march of human progress and had
not yet regained its place. Addressing the graduating class at the University of Alabama in 1884,
he faced the issue squarely, declaring that the
Negroes suffered gross abridgment of their rights
and asking that they be given the justice he was
convinced they did not receive in the courts. Although he knew what such a plea would cost him
in public favor — as newspaper editorials made
clear at once — and how much it would handicap
his other reform efforts, he felt compelled to speak
out. Any hesitation he might have had about further
steps was removed when an opportunity came to
present his case before a national audience and
thus to gain more support, he hoped, than would
have been possible otherwise. Earlier than his address at Louisville he had appeared as a social reformer outside his own region; he had spoken on
prison reform before the Congregational Club of
New York, March 26, 1883, and had met Morris
K. Jessup, William E. Dodge, and others identified
with programs for social improvement. Now he
was invited to address the National Social Science
Association meeting in Saratoga, New York, September 11, 1884, where he spoke on "The Freedman's Case in Equity."

Cable presented the "freedman's case" because

he believed that not to do so would be criminal, and
near the end of the essay he asked, "Is it not well to
have done so?" Noting that he was the son and
grandson of slaveholders, had fought in the Confederate army, and therefore had strong ties of
affection and loyalty to his region, he nevertheless
asked the South to give up its doctrines of class and
caste, white superiority and white supremacy. Such
generalized urging as this, Cable knew, might draw
only generalized rejoinders and be largely ignored.
Determined to make the case impressive enough to
call out remedial action, he recounted the pathetic
and absurd incident he had witnessed on a train in
Alabama, when a well-dressed Negro mother and
her child were required to leave the car for whites
and ride with a company of Negro convicts being
transported in chains from the mines. He remarked
on the general exclusion of Negroes from juries
and the paucity of funds for needed public im-
provements, and he added, "we may almost assert
beforehand that the popular mind will — not so
maliciously as unreflectingly — yield to the tremendous temptation to hustle the misbehaving black
man into the State prison under extravagant sentence, and sell his labor to the highest bidder who
will use him in the construction of public works."
The official penitentiary reports themselves, he
said, proved this assertion to be correct.

The Federal government, Cable realized, had

largely withdrawn its authority, leaving the solution of the race question to the South. He did not
protest, for he was confident that Southerners,
with the issues laid out clearly before them, would
respond with justice and humanity. Spokesmen for
the region, however, especially newspaper editors
and politicians, raised such a cry, attacking Cable
with every weapon from solemn questioning of his
information and his motives to crude name-calling,
that the broad public had no opportunity to respond, or even to judge the issues he undertook to
explain. Henry W. Grady, editor of the Atlanta
Constitution, champion of a New South of diversi-
fication and industry, and advocate of reconcilia-
tion between the North and the South, wrote for
Century Magazine what the editors considered a
reply to Cable for those in the South who opposed
his views. Believing that Grady did not speak for
the entire South in his emotional pleas for white
supremacy, Cable wrote for the September issue of
Century his most carefully reasoned essay on the
subject. He chose the title "The Silent South" to
indicate his belief that there did indeed exist a great
voiceless, silent South for which he might speak in
a voice of justice, reason, compassion, and practical humanity.

Never doubting the efficacy of open discussion,
Cable proposed including Grady's essay in *Century*
along with his own essays, but his publisher,

Charles Scribner, discouraged the idea. When a new edition of *The Silent South* appeared in 1889, however, two magazine pieces by others in the debate, John W. Johnston and A. E. Orr, were included, along with Cable's replies. It was as an introduction to this new edition that he wrote "My Politics," which he intended as an autobiographical account that would reply to the charges being made against him. His publishers thought the account should not be published, and it was laid away.

"The Freedman's Case in Equity" and "The Silent South" asserted the broad principles on which Cable stood and his main arguments in the controversy over Negro rights. For several years afterward he continued to advance his views in lectures and essays and in the Open Letter Club, an informal group of Southerners he organized to exchange ideas in letters and essays and to publish the conclusions they reached, whether in agreement or disagreement, on aspects of the Southern question. The titles of Cable's later essays suggest his persistence in the discussion: "The Negro Question," "What Makes the Color Line?" "What Shall the Negro Do?" "What the Negro Must Learn," "Does the Negro Pay for His Education?" "National Aid to Southern Schools," "Congregational Unity in Georgia." Several times he addressed Negro audiences and afterward published the addresses. He urged them to vote at whatever cost, not to sell their ballots for delivered or promised benefits, never to accept anything less than full citizenship, to seek improved education and to develop their own leaders. Cable recognized that most arguments for states rights were false, for the real objection was most often the substance of the action in question, not the agent. He believed the Federal government had an obligation to help finance education for the Negroes and also to ensure that states or other political units did not deprive any citizens of their rights.

Whatever he said of the Negroes, Cable declared again and again, applied to the white poor also, only to a lesser degree. The poor had less chance than the rich of securing justice in the courts, less chance of receiving a good education, less chance of enjoying full public rights. He wrote primarily about the Negro, Cable said, because the Negro was beyond all others the South's poor man. Similarly he noted the nation's disgrace in dealing with the American Indians, but added that their numbers were relatively small. Again, Negroes experienced abridgment of rights in the North, but most of them lived in the South — and since he was himself a Southerner hoping to improve his own region, his efforts had to be focused there.

Cable published a collection of these later essays in *The Negro Question* (1890). Among papers in the Cable Collection at Tulane University are several fragments, especially on education in the South, which he left unfinished when magazine editors were no longer interested in publishing his controversial writings. He had moved from the South, and in 1885 had settled in Northampton, Massachusetts. Two years later he inaugurated in his new home a program for social and cultural betterment, the Home Culture Clubs, and afterward a garden club competition, both of which proved highly successful and held his attention the rest of his life. He regretted that he could no longer work directly for reform in the South, but he often had something to say on Southern topics. His last novel, *Lovers of Louisiana* (1918), took up again the questions of race and class and advanced the same views its author held thirty-five years earlier. Cable still had faith that the reforms he had championed would be achieved.

Selected Bibliography

BOOKS BY CABLE

(Published by Charles Scribner's Sons except as indicated.)

Old Creole Days, 1879

The Grandissimes, 1880

Madame Delphine, 1881

The Creoles of Louisiana, 1884

Dr. Sevier, 1884 (Boston: J. R. Osgood and Company)

The Silent South, 1885 (expanded edition, 1889)

Bonaventure, 1888

Strange True Stories of Louisiana, 1889

The Negro Question, 1890

The Busy Man's Bible, 1891 (Meadville, Pa.: Chautauqua-Century Press)

A Memory of Roswell Smith, [1892] (privately printed)

John March, Southerner, 1894

Strong Hearts, 1899

The Cavalier, 1901

Bylow Hill, 1902

Kincaid's Battery, 1908

Posson Jone' and Père Raphaël, 1909

Gideon's Band, 1914

The Amateur Garden, 1914

The Flower of the Chapdelaines, 1918

Lovers of Louisiana, 1918

COLLECTIONS OF CABLE'S WRITINGS

A Southerner Looks at Negro Discrimination: Selected Writings of George W. Cable, ed. Isabel Cable Manes (New York: International Publishers, 1946)

Twins of Genius, ed. Guy A. Cardwell (East Lansing: Michigan State University Press, 1953)

The Negro Question: A Selection of Writings on Civil Rights in the South by George W. Cable, ed. Arlin Turner (Garden City: Doubleday and Company, 1958; New York: W. W. Norton, 1968)

Creoles and Cajuns: Stories of Old Louisiana by George W. Cable, ed. Arlin Turner (Garden City: Doubleday and Company, 1959)

Mark Twain and George W. Cable: The Record of a Literary Friendship, ed. Arlin Turner (East Lansing: Michigan State University Press, 1960)

WORKS DEALING WITH CABLE

Baskervill, William M., *Southern Writers* (Nashville: Publishing House, Methodist Episcopal Church, South, 1897-1903), I, 299-356

Biklé, Lucy L. C., *George W. Cable: His Life and Letters* (New York: Charles Scribner's Sons, 1928)

Butcher, Philip, *George W. Cable: The Northampton Years* (New York: Columbia University Press, 1959)

Butcher, Philip, *George W. Cable* (New York: Twayne Publishers, 1962)

Dennis, Mary Cable, *The Tail of the Comet* (New York: E. P. Dutton, 1937)

Ekström, Kjell, *George Washington Cable: A Study of His Early Life and Work* (Upsala: Lundequistska Bokhandeln; Cambridge, Mass.: Harvard University Press, 1950)

Turner, Arlin, *George W. Cable: A Biography* (Durham, N. C.: Duke University Press, 1956; Baton Rouge: Louisiana State University Press, 1966)

Wilson, Edmund, "The Ordeal of George Washington Cable," *New Yorker,* XXXIII (November 9, 1957), 172-216

Wilson, Edmund, *Patriotic Gore* (New York: Oxford University Press, 1962), pp. 548-587

PREFACE TO THE 1889 EDITION

When the following essays first appeared in
book form (1885) they entered a vacant field.
The equities and ethics of the " Southern Question " were not at all then, as now so widely they
are, current themes of discussion in literary form.
In seeing a new edition go to press, the author
finds occasion to say only that whatever value
originally attached to these pages he claims for
them still, as he is not aware of any effort having
been made in the spirit of serious debate, since
their first issue in book form, to answer the statements either of conditions or principles here set
forth; save only the " Open Letters " [CENTURY
MAGAZINE, May–October, 1886] of ex-Senator
John W. Johnston, of Richmond, Virginia, and
Mr. A. E. Orr, of Atlanta, Georgia, which, with
my replies, are to be found at the end of this
volume.

G. W. CABLE.

THE FREEDMAN'S CASE IN EQUITY

THE FREEDMAN'S CASE IN EQUITY.

I. THE NATION'S ATTITUDE.

THE greatest social problem before the American people to-day is, as it has been for a hundred years, the presence among us of the negro.

No comparable entanglement was ever drawn round itself by any other modern nation with so serene a disregard of its ultimate issue, or with a more distinct national responsibility. The African slave was brought here by cruel force, and with everybody's consent except his own. Everywhere the practice was favored as a measure of common aggrandizement. When a few men and women protested, they were mobbed in the public interest, with the public consent. There rests, therefore, a moral responsibility on the whole nation never to lose sight of the results of African-American slavery until they cease to work mischief and injustice.

It is true these responsibilities may not fall everywhere with the same weight; but they are nowhere entirely removed. The original seed of trouble was sown with the full knowledge and

consent of the nation.   The nation was to blame;
and so long as evils spring from it, their correction must be the nation's duty.

The late Southern slave has within two decades
risen from slavery to freedom, from freedom to
citizenship, passed on into political ascendency,
and fallen again from that eminence.   The
amended Constitution holds him up in his new
political rights as well as a mere constitution can.
On the other hand, certain enactments of Congress, trying to reach further, have lately been
made void by the highest court of the nation.
And another thing has happened.   The popular
mind in the old free States, weary of strife at
arm's length, bewildered by its complications,
vexed by many a blunder, eager to turn to the
cure of other evils, and even tinctured by that
race feeling whose grosser excesses it would so
gladly see suppressed, has retreated from its uncomfortable dictational attitude and thrown the
whole matter over to the States of the South.
Here it rests, no longer a main party issue, but a
group of questions which are to be settled by
each of these States separately in the light of
simple equity and morals, and which the genius
of American government is at least loath to
force upon them from beyond their borders.
Thus the whole question, become secondary in
party contest, has yet reached a period of su-
preme importance.

II. OLD SOUTH AND NEW.

Before slavery ever became a grave question in the nation's politics,—when it seemed each State's private affair, developing unmolested,—it had two different fates in two different parts of the country. In one, treated as a question of public equity, it withered away. In the other, overlooked in that aspect, it petrified and became the corner-stone of the whole social structure; and when men sought its overthrow as a national evil, it first brought war upon the land, and then grafted into the citizenship of one of the most intelligent nations in the world six millions of people from one of the most debased races on the globe.

And now this painful and wearisome question, sown in the African slave-trade, reaped in our civil war, and garnered in the national adoption of millions of an inferior race, is drawing near a second seed-time. For this is what the impatient proposal to make it a dead and buried issue really means. It means to recommit it to the silence and concealment of the covered furrow. Beyond that incubative retirement no suppressed moral question can be pushed; but all such questions, ignored in the domain of private morals, spring up and expand once more into questions of public equity; neglected as matters of public equity, they blossom into questions of national interest; and, despised in that guise, presently yield the red fruits of revolution.

This question must never again bear that fruit. There must arise, nay, there has arisen, in the South itself, a desire to see established the equities of the issue ; to make it no longer a question of endurance between one group of States and another, but between the moral débris of an exploded evil, and the duty, necessity, and value of planting society firmly upon universal justice and equity. This, and this only, can give the matter final burial. True, it is still a question between States; but only secondarily, as something formerly participated in, or as it concerns every householder to know that what is being built against his house is built by level and plummet. It is the interest of the Southern States first, and *consequently* of the whole land, to discover clearly these equities and the errors that are being committed against them.

If we take up this task, the difficulties of the situation are plain. We have, first, a revision of Southern State laws which has forced into them the recognition of certain human rights discordant with the sentiments of those who have always called themselves the community; second, the removal of the entire political machinery by which this forcing process was effected; and, third, these revisions left to be interpreted and applied under the domination of these antago-

nistic sentiments. These being the three terms
of the problem, one of three things must result.
There will arise a system of vicious evasions
eventually ruinous to public and private morals
and liberty, or there will be a candid reconsider-
ation of the sentiments hostile to these enactments, or else there will be a division, some taking one course and some the other.

This is what we should look for from our
knowledge of men and history; and this is what
we find. The revised laws, only where they
could not be evaded, have met that reluctant or
simulated acceptance of their narrowest letter
which might have been expected—a virtual suf-
focation of those principles of human equity
which the unwelcome decrees do little more than
shadow forth. But in different regions this attitude has been made in very different degrees of
emphasis. In some the new principles have
grown, or are growing, into the popular conviction, and the opposing sentiments are correspond-
ingly dying out. There are even some districts
where they have received much practical acceptance. While, again, other limited sections lean
almost wholly toward the old sentiments; an
easy choice, since it is the conservative, the un-
yielding attitude, whose strength is in the absence of intellectual and moral debate.

Now, what are the gains, what the losses of
these diverse attitudes? Surely these are urgent

questions to any one in our country who be-
lieves it is always a losing business to be in the
wrong.   Particularly in the South, where each
step in this affair is an unprecedented experience,
it will be folly if each region, small or large, does
not study the experiences of all the rest.   And
yet this, alone, would be superficial; we should
still need to do more.   We need to go back to
the roots of things and study closely, analytically,
the origin, the present foundation. the rationality,
the rightness, of those sentiments surviving in
us which prompt an attitude qualifying in any
way peculiarly the black man's liberty among us.
Such a treatment will be less abundant in incident, less picturesque ; but it will be more
thorough.

III. THE ROOTS OF THE QUESTION.

First, then, what are these sentiments ?   Foremost among them stands the idea that he is of
necessity an alien.   He was brought to our
shores a naked, brutish, unclean, captive, pagan
savage,[1] to be and remain a kind of connecting
link between man and the beasts of burden.   The
great changes to result from his contact with a
superb race of masters were not taken into account.   As a social factor he was intended to be
as purely zero as the brute at the other end of
his plow-line.   The occasional mingling of his
blood with that of the white man worked no

[1] Sometimes he was not a mere savage but a trading, smithing,
weaving, town-building, crop-raising barbarian.

change in the sentiment; one, two, four, eight, multiplied upon or divided into zero, still gave zero for the result. Generations of American nativity made no difference; his children and children's children were born in sight of our door, yet the old notion held fast. He increased to vast numbers, but it never wavered. He accepted our dress, language, religion, all the fundamentals of our civilization, and became forever expatriated from his own land; still he remained, to us, an alien. Our sentiment went blind. It did not see that gradually, here by force and there by choice, he was fulfilling a host of conditions that earned at least a solemn moral right to that naturalization which no one at first had dreamed of giving him. Frequently he even bought back the freedom of which he had been robbed, became a tax-payer, and at times an educator of his children at his own expense; but the old idea of alienism passed laws to banish him, his wife, and children by thousands from the State, and threw him into loathsome jails as a common felon, for returning to his native land.[1]

It will be wise to remember that these were the acts of an enlightened, God-fearing people, the great mass of whom have passed beyond all earthly accountability. They were our fathers. I am the son and grandson of slave-holders. These were their faults; posterity will discover ours; but these things must be frankly, fearlessly

[1] Notably in Louisiana in 1810 and subsequently.

taken into account if we are ever to understand the true interests of our peculiar state of society.

Why, then, did this notion, that the man of color must always remain an alien, stand so unshaken? We may readily recall how, under ancient systems, he rose not only to high privileges, but often to public station and power. Singularly, with us the trouble lay in a modern principle of liberty. The whole idea of American government rested on all men's equal, inalienable right to secure their life, liberty, and the pursuit of happiness by governments founded in their own consent. Hence, our Southern forefathers, shedding their blood, or ready to shed it, for this principle, yet proposing in equal good conscience to continue holding the American black man and mulatto and quadroon in slavery, had to anchor that conscience, their conduct, and their laws in the conviction that the man of African tincture was, not by his master's arbitrary assertion merely, but by nature and unalterably, an alien. If that hold should break, one single wave of irresistible inference would lift our whole Southern social fabric and dash it upon the rocks of negro emancipation and enfranchisement. How was it made secure? Not by books, though they were written among us from every possible point of view, but, with the mass of our slave-owners, by the calm hypothesis of a positive, intuitive knowledge. To them the statement was

an axiom. They abandoned the methods of
moral and intellectual reasoning, and fell back
upon this assumption of a God-given instinct,
nobler than reason, and which it was an insult
to a freeman to ask him to prove on logical
grounds.

Yet it was found not enough. The slave multiplied. Slavery was a dangerous institution.
Few in the South to-day have any just idea how
often the slave plotted for his freedom. Our
Southern ancestors were a noble, manly people,
springing from some of the most highly intelligent, aspiring, upright, and refined nations of the
modern world ; from the Huguenot, the French
Chevalier, the Old Englander, the New Englander. Their acts were not always right ; whose
are ? But for their peace of mind they had to
believe them so. They therefore spoke much of
the negro's contentment with that servile condition for which nature had designed him. Yet
there was no escaping the knowledge that we
dared not trust the slave caste with any power
that could be withheld from them. So the perpetual alien was made also a perpetual menial,
and the belief became fixed that this, too, was
nature's decree, not ours.

Thus we stood at the close of the civil war.
There were always a few Southerners who did
not justify slavery, and many who cared nothing
whether it was just or not. But what we have

described was the general sentiment of good
Southern people.   There was one modifying
sentiment.   It related to the slave's spiritual
interests.   Thousands of pious masters and mis-
tresses flatly broke the shameful laws that stood
between their slaves and the Bible.   Slavery was
right; but religion, they held, was for the alien
and menial as well as for the citizen and master.
They could be alien and citizen, menial and
master, in church as well as out; and they
were.

Yet over against this lay another root of to-
day's difficulties.   This perpetuation of the alien,
menial relation tended to perpetuate the vices
that naturally cling to servility, dense ignorance
and a hopeless separation from true liberty ; and
as we could not find it in our minds to blame
slavery with this perpetuation, we could only
assume as a further axiom that there was, by
nature, a disqualifying moral taint in every drop
of negro blood.   The testimony of an Irish,
German, Italian, French, or Spanish beggar in a
court of justice was taken on its merits ; but the
colored man's was excluded by law wherever it
weighed against a white man.   The colored man
was a prejudged culprit.   The discipline of the
plantation required that the difference between
master and slave be never lost sight of by either.
It made our master caste a solid mass, and fixed
a common masterhood and subserviency between

the ruling and the serving race.[1] Every one of us grew up in the idea that he had, by birth and race, certain broad powers of police over any and every person of color.

All at once the tempest of war snapped off at the ground every one of these arbitrary relations, without removing a single one of the sentiments in which they stood rooted. Then, to fortify the freedman in the tenure of his new rights, he was given the ballot. Before this grim fact the notion of alienism, had it been standing alone, might have given way. The idea that slavery was right did begin to crumble almost at once. " As for slavery," said an old Creole sugar-planter and former slave-owner to me, " it was damnable." The revelation came like a sudden burst of light. It is one of the South's noblest poets who has but just said :

> " I am a Southerner ;
> I love the South ; I dared for her
> To fight from Lookout to the sea,
> With her proud banner over me :
> But from my lips thanksgiving broke,
> As God in battle-thunder spoke,
> And that Black Idol, breeding drouth
> And dearth of human sympathy

[1] The old Louisiana Black Code says, " That free people **of** color ought never to . . . presume to conceive themselves equal to the white ; but, on the contrary, that they ought to yield to them in every occasion, and never speak or answer to them but with respect, under the penalty of imprisonment according to the nature of the offense." (Section 21, p. 164.)

Throughout the sweet and sensuous South,
    Was, with its chains and human yoke,
Blown hellward from the cannon's mouth,
    While Freedom cheered behind the smoke!"[1]

IV. WHAT THE WAR LEFT.

With like readiness might the old alien relation have given way if we could only, while
letting that pass, have held fast by the other old
ideas. But they were all bound together. See
our embarrassment. For more than a hundred
years we had made these sentiments the absolute
essentials to our self-respect. And yet if we
clung to them, how could we meet the freedman
on equal terms in the political field? Even to
lead would not compensate us; for the fundamental profession of American politics is that
the leader is servant to his followers. It was too
much. The ex-master and ex-slave—the quarter-
deck and the forecastle, as it were—could not
come together. But neither could the American
mind tolerate a continuance of martial law. The
agonies of Reconstruction followed.

The vote, after all, was a secondary point, and
the robbery and bribery on one side, and whipping and killing on the other, were but huge
accidents of the situation. The two main questions were really these : on the freedman's side,
how to establish republican State government

[1] Maurice Thompson, in the "Independent."

under the same recognition of his rights that the rest of Christendom accorded him ; and on the former master's side, how to get back to the old semblance of republican State government, and —allowing that the freedman was *de facto* a voter—still to maintain a purely arbitrary superiority of all whites over all blacks, and a purely arbitrary equality of all blacks among themselves as an alien, menial, and dangerous class.

Exceptionally here and there some one in the master caste did throw off the old and accept the new ideas, and, if he would allow it, was instantly claimed as a leader by the newly liberated thousands around him. But just as promptly the old master race branded him also an alien reprobate, and in ninety-nine cases out of a hundred, if he had not already done so, he soon began to confirm by his actions the brand on his cheek. However, we need give no history here of the dreadful episode of Reconstruction. Under an experimentative truce its issues rest to-day upon the pledge of the wiser leaders of the master class : Let us but remove the hireling demagogue, and we will see to it that the freedman is accorded a practical, complete, and cordial recognition of his equality with the white man before the law. As far as there has been any understanding at all, it is not that the originally desired ends of reconstruction have been abandoned, but that the men of North and South have agreed upon a new, gentle, and peaceable method for reaching them ; that, without change as to the ends in view, compulsory reconstruction has been set aside and a voluntary reconstruction is on trial.

It is the fashion to say we paused to let the " feelings engendered by the war " pass away, and that they are passing. But let not these truths lead us into error. The sentiments we have been analyzing, and upon which we saw the old compulsory reconstruction go hard aground— these are not the "feelings engendered by the war." We must disentangle them from the " feelings engendered by the war," and by reconstruction. They are older than either. But for them slavery would have perished of itself, and emancipation and reconstruction been peaceful revolutions.

Indeed, as between master and slave, the "feelings engendered by the war," are too trivial, or at least were too short-lived, to demand our present notice. One relation and feeling the war destroyed : the patriarchal tie and its often really tender and benevolent sentiment of dependence and protection. When the slave became a freedman, the sentiment of alienism became for the first time complete. The abandonment of this relation was not one-sided; the slave, even before the master, renounced it. Countless times, since reconstruction began, the master has tried, in what he believed to be everybody's interest, to

play on that old sentiment. But he found it a
harp without strings. The freedman could not
formulate, but he could see, all our old ideas of
autocracy and subserviency, of master and menial,
of an arbitrarily fixed class to guide and rule,
and another to be guided and ruled. He rejected
the overture. The old master, his well-meant
condescensions slighted, turned away estranged,
and justified himself in passively withholding that
simpler protection without patronage which any
one American citizen, however exalted, owes to
any other, however humble. Could the freedman
in the bitterest of those days have consented to
throw himself upon just that one old relation, he
could have found a physical security for himself
and his house such as could not, after years of
effort, be given him by constitutional amendments, Congress, United States marshals, regi-
ments of regulars, and ships of war. But he
could not; the very nobility of the civilization
that had held him in slavery had made him too
much a man to go back to that shelter; and by
his manly neglect to do so he has proved to us
who once ruled over him that, be his relative
standing among the races of men what it may, he
is worthy to be free.

V. FREED——NOT FREE.

To be a free man is his still distant goal.   Twice
he has been a freedman.   In the days of compulsory reconstruction he was freed in the presence
of his master by that master's victorious foe.   In
these days of voluntary reconstruction he is virtually freed by the consent of his master, but the
master retaining the exclusive right to define the
bounds of his freedom.   Many everywhere have
taken up the idea that this state of affairs is the
end to be desired and the end actually sought in
reconstruction as handed over to the States.   I
do not charge such folly to the best intelligence
of any American community; but I cannot ignore
my own knowledge that the average thought of
some regions rises to no better idea of the issue.
The belief is all too common that the nation,
having aimed at a wrong result and missed, has
left us of the Southern States to get now such
other result as we think best.   I say this belief is
not universal.   There are those among us who
see that America has no room for a state of society which makes its lower classes harmless by
abridging their liberties, or, as one of the favored
class lately said to me, has "got 'em so they don't
give no trouble."   There is a growing number
who see that the one thing we cannot afford to
tolerate at large is a class of people less than citizens; and that every interest in the land demands

that the freedman be free to become in all things, as far as his own personal gifts will lift and sustain him, the same sort of American citizen he would be if, with the same intellectual and moral calibre, he were white.

Thus we reach the ultimate question of fact. Are the freedman's liberties suffering any real abridgment? The answer is easy. The letter of the laws, with a few exceptions, recognizes him as entitled to every right of an American citizen; and to some it may seem unimportant that there is scarcely one public relation of life in the South where he is not arbitrarily and unlawfully compelled to hold toward the white man the attitude of an alien, a menial, and a probable reprobate, by reason of his race and color. One of the marvels of future history will be that it was counted a small matter, by a majority of our nation, for six millions of people within it, made by its own decree a component part of it, to be subjected to a system of oppression so rank that nothing could make it seem small except the fact that they had already been ground under it for a century and a half.

Examine it. It proffers to the freedman a certain security of life and property, and then holds the respect of the community, that dearest of earthly boons, beyond his attainment. It gives him certain guarantees against thieves and robbers, and then holds him under the unearned contumely of the mass of good men and women. It acknowledges in constitutions and statutes his title to an American's freedom and aspirations, and then in daily practice heaps upon him in every public place the most odious distinctions, without giving ear to the humblest plea concerning mental or moral character. It spurns his ambition, tramples upon his languishing self-respect, and indignantly refuses to let him either buy with money, or earn by any excellence of inner life or outward behavior, the most momentary immunity from these public indignities even for his wife and daughters. Need we cram these pages with facts in evidence, as if these were charges denied and requiring to be proven? They are simply the present avowed and defended state of affairs peeled of its exteriors.

Nothing but the habit, generations old, of enduring it could make it endurable by men not in actual slavery. Were we whites of the South to remain every way as we are, and our six million blacks to give place to any sort of whites exactly their equals, man for man, in mind, morals, and wealth, provided only that they had tasted two years of American freedom, and were this same system of tyrannies attempted upon them, there would be as bloody an uprising as this continent has ever seen. We can say this quietly. There is not a scruple's weight of present danger. These six million freedmen are dominated by

nine million whites immeasurably stronger than
they, backed by the virtual consent of thirty odd
millions more. Indeed, nothing but the habit
of oppression could make such oppression possible to a people of the intelligence and virtue
of our Southern whites, and the invitation to
practice it on millions of any other than the
children of their former slaves would be spurned
with a noble indignation.

Suppose, for a moment, the tables turned.
Suppose the courts of our Southern States, while
changing no laws requiring the impaneling of
jurymen without distinction as to race, etc.,
should suddenly begin to draw their thousands
of jurymen all black, and well-nigh every one of
them counting not only himself, but all his race,
better than any white man. Assuming that their
average of intelligence and morals should be not
below that of jurymen as now drawn, would a
white man, for all that, choose to be tried in one
of those courts? Would he suspect nothing?
Could one persuade him that his chances of even
justice were all they should be, or all they would
be were the court not evading the law in order
to sustain an outrageous distinction against him
because of the accidents of his birth? Yet only
read white man for black man, and black man for
white man, and that—I speak as an eye-witness—
has been the practice for years, and is still so to-
day; an actual emasculation, in the case of six

million people both as plaintiff and defendant, of the right of trial by jury.

In this and other practices the outrage falls upon the freedman. Does it stop there? Far from it. It is the first premise of American principles that whatever elevates the lower stratum of the people lifts all the rest, and whatever holds it down holds all down. For twenty years, therefore, the nation has been working to elevate the freedman. It counts this one of the great necessities of the hour. It has poured out its wealth publicly and privately for this purpose. It is confidently hoped that it will soon bestow a royal gift of millions for the reduction of the illiteracy so largely shared by the blacks. Our Southern States are, and for twenty years have been, taxing themselves for the same end. The private charities alone of the other States have given twenty millions in the same good cause. Their colored seminaries, colleges, and normal schools dot our whole Southern country, and furnish our public colored schools with a large part of their teachers. All this and much more has been or is being done in order that, for the good of himself and everybody else in the land, the colored man may be elevated as quickly as possible from all the debasements of slavery and semi-slavery to the full stature and integrity of citizenship. And it is in the face of all this that the adherent of the old régime stands in the way

to every public privilege and place—steamer
landing, railway platform, theatre, concert-hall,
art display, public library, public school, courthouse, church, everything—flourishing the hot
branding-iron of ignominious distinctions. He
forbids the freedman to go into the water until *he*
is satisfied that he knows how to swim, and for
fear he should learn hangs mill-stones about his
neck. This is what we are told is a small matter
that will settle itself. Yes, like a roosting curse,
until the outraged intelligence of the South lifts
its indignant protest against this stupid firing into
our own ranks.

VI. ITS DAILY WORKINGS.

I say the outraged intelligence of the South;
for there are thousands of Southern-born white
men and women, in the minority in all these
places—in churches, courts, schools, libraries,
theatres, concert-halls, and on steamers and railway carriages,—who see the wrong and folly of
these things, silently blush for them, and withhold their open protests only because their belief
is unfortunately stronger in the futility of their
counsel than in the power of a just cause. I do
not justify their silence; but I affirm their sincerity and their goodly numbers. Of late years,
when condemning these evils from the platform
in Southern towns, I have repeatedly found that
those who I had earlier been told were the men

and women in whom the community placed most confidence and pride—they were the ones who, when I had spoken, came forward with warmest hand-grasps and expressions of thanks, and pointedly and cordially justified my every utterance. And were they the young South? Not by half. The gray-beards of the old times have always been among them, saying in effect, not by any means as converts, but as fellow-discoverers, "Whereas we were blind, now we see."

Another sort among our good Southern people make a similar but feeble admission, but with the time-worn proviso that expediency makes a more imperative demand than law, justice, or logic, and demands the preservation of the old order. Somebody must be outraged, it seems; and if not the freedman, then it must be a highly refined and enlightened race of people constantly offended and grossly discommoded, if not imposed upon, by a horde of tatterdemalions, male and female, crowding into a participation in their reserved privileges. Now, look at this plea. It is simply saying in another way that though the Southern whites far outnumber the blacks, and though we hold every element of power in greater degree than the blacks, and though the larger part of us claim to be sealed by nature as an exclusive upper class, and though we have the courts completely in our own hands, with the police on our right and the prisons on our left, and though we justly claim to be an intrepid people, and though we have a superb military experience, with ninety-nine hundredths of all the military equipment and no scarcity of all the accessories, yet with all these facts behind us we cannot make and enforce that intelligent and approximately just assortment of persons in public places and conveyances on the merits of exterior decency that is made in all other enlightened lands. On such a plea are made a distinction and separation that not only are crude, invidious, humiliating, and tyrannous, but which do not reach their ostensible end or come near it; and all that saves such a plea from being a confession of driveling imbecility is its utter speciousness. It is advanced sincerely; and yet nothing is easier to show than that these distinctions on the line of color are really made not from any necessity, but simply for their own sake—to preserve the old arbitrary supremacy of the master class over the menial without regard to the decency or indecency of appearance or manners in either the white individual or the colored.

See its every-day working. Any colored man gains unquestioned admission into innumerable places the moment he appears as the menial attendant of some white person, where he could not cross the threshold in his own right as a well-dressed and well-behaved master of himself. The contrast is even greater in the case of colored women. There could not be a system which when put into practice would more offensively condemn itself. It does more : it actually creates the confusion it pretends to prevent. It blunts the sensibilities of the ruling class themselves. It waives all strict demand for painstaking in either manners or dress of either master or menial, and, for one result, makes the average Southern railway coach more uncomfortable than the average of railway coaches elsewhere. It prompts the average Southern white passenger to find less offense in the presence of a profane, boisterous, or unclean white person than in that of a quiet, well-behaved colored man or woman attempting to travel on an equal footing with him without a white master or mistress. The holders of the old sentiments hold the opposite choice in scorn. It is only when we go on to say that there are regions where the riotous expulsion of a decent and peaceable colored person is preferred to his inoffensive company, that it may seem necessary to bring in evidence. And yet here again it is *prima facie* evidence; for the following extract was printed in the Selma (Alabama) "Times" not six months ago,[1] and not as a complaint, but as a boast :

"A few days since, a negro minister, of this city, boarded the east-bound passenger train on the E. T., V. & G. Railway and

[1] In the summer of 1884.

took a seat in the coach occupied by white passengers. Some of the passengers complained to the conductor and brakemen, and expressed considerable dissatisfaction that they were forced to ride alongside of a negro. The railroad officials informed the complainants that they were not authorized to force the colored passenger into the coach set apart for the negroes, and they would lay themselves liable should they do so. The white passengers then took the matter in their own hands and ordered the ebony-hued minister to take a seat in the next coach. He positively refused to obey orders, whereupon the white men gave him a sound flogging and forced him to a seat among his own color and equals. We learned yesterday that the vanquished preacher was unable to fill his pulpit on account of the severe chastisement inflicted upon him. Now [says the delighted editor] the query that puzzles is, ' Who did the flogging ? ' "

And as good an answer as we can give is that likely enough they were some of the men for whom the whole South has come to a halt to let them get over the " feelings engendered by the war." Must such men, such acts, such sentiments, stand alone to represent us of the South before an enlightened world ? No. I say, as a citizen of an extreme Southern State, a native of Louisiana, an ex-Confederate soldier, and a lover of my home, my city, and my State, as well as of my country, that this is not the best sentiment in the South, nor the sentiment of her best intelligence ; and that it would not ride up and down that beautiful land dominating and domineering were it not for its tremendous power as the *traditional* sentiment of a conservative people. But is not silent endurance criminal ? I cannot but repeat my own words, spoken near the scene and about the time of this event. Speech may be silvern and silence golden ; but if a lump of gold is only big enough, it can drag us to the bottom of the sea and hold us there while all the world sails over us.

The laws passed in the days of compulsory reconstruction requiring " equal accommodations," etc., for colored and white persons were freedmen's follies. On their face they defeated their ends ; for even in theory they at once reduced to half all opportunity for those more reasonable and mutually agreeable self-assortments which public assemblages and groups of passengers find it best to make in all other enlightened countries, making them on the score of conduct, dress, and price. They also led the whites to overlook what they would have seen instantly had these invidious distinctions been made against themselves : that their offense does not vanish at the guarantee against the loss of physical comforts. But we made, and are still making, a mistake beyond even this. For years many of us have carelessly taken for granted that these laws were being carried out in some shape that removed all just ground of complaint. It is common to say, " We allow the man of color to go and come at will, only let him sit apart in a place marked off for him." But marked off how ? So as to mark him instantly as a menial. Not by railings and partitions merely, which, raised

against any other class in the United States with
the same invidious intent, would be kicked down
as fast as put up, but by giving him besides, in
every instance and without recourse, the most
uncomfortable, uncleanest, and unsafest place ;
and the unsafety, uncleanness, and discomfort of
most of these places are a shame to any community pretending to practice public justice. If
any one can think the freedman does not feel the
indignities thus heaped upon him, let him take
up any paper printed for colored men's patronage,
or ask any colored man of known courageous
utterance. Hear them :

"We ask not Congress, nor the Legislature, nor any other
power, to remedy these evils, but we ask the people among whom
we live. Those who *can* remedy them if they *will*. Those who
have a high sense of honor and a deep moral feeling. Those
who have one vestige of human sympathy left. . . . Those are
the ones we ask to protect us in our weakness and ill-treatments.
. . . As soon as the colored man is treated by the white man as
a *man*, that harmony and pleasant feeling which should charac·
terize all races which dwell together, shall be the bond of peace
between them."

Surely their evidence is good enough to prove
their own feelings. We need not lean upon it
here for anything else. I shall not bring forward
a single statement of fact from them or any of
their white friends who, as teachers and mission-
aries, share many of their humiliations, though
my desk is covered with them. But I beg to
make the same citation from my own experience

that I made last June[1] in the far South.   It was
this: One hot night in September of last year[2] I
was traveling by rail in the State of Alabama.
At rather late bed-time there came aboard the
train a young mother and her little daughter of
three or four years.   They were neatly and taste-
fully dressed in cool, fresh muslins, and as the
train went on its way they sat together very still
and quiet.   At the next station there came aboard
a most melancholy and revolting company.   In
filthy rags, with vile odors and the clanking of
shackles and chains, nine penitentiary convicts
chained to one chain, and ten more chained
to another, dragged laboriously into the com-
partment of the car where in one corner sat
this mother and child, and packed it full, and the
train moved on.   The keeper of the convicts told
me he should take them in that car two hundred
miles that night.   They were going to the mines.
My seat was not in that car, and I staid in it but
a moment.   It stank insufferably.   I returned to
my own place in the coach behind, where there
was, and had all the time been, plenty of room.
But the mother and child sat on in silence in that
foul hole, the conductor having distinctly refused
them admission elsewhere because they were of
African blood, and not because the mother was,
but because she was *not*, engaged at the moment
in menial service.   Had the child been white, and
the mother not its natural but its hired guardian,

    [1] 1884.   [2] 1883.

she could have sat anywhere in the train, and no
one would have ventured to object, even had she
been as black as the mouth of the coal-pit to
which her loathsome fellow-passengers were being
carried in chains.

Such is the incident as I saw it. But the illus-
tration would be incomplete here were I not
allowed to add the comments I made upon it
when in June last I recounted it, and to state the
two opposite tempers in which my words were
received. I said: " These are the facts. And
yet you know and I know we belong to communities that after years of hoping for, are at last
taking comfort in the assurance of the nation's
highest courts that no law can reach and stop
this shameful foul play until we choose to enact
a law to that end ourselves. And now the east
and north and west of our great and prosperous
and happy country, and the rest of the civilized
world, as far as it knows our case, are standing
and waiting to see what we will write upon the
white page of to-day's and to-morrow's history,
now that we are simply on our honor and on the
mettle of our far and peculiarly famed Southern
instinct. How long, then, shall we stand off from
such ringing moral questions as these on the
flimsy plea that they have a political value, and,
scrutinizing the Constitution, keep saying, ' Is it
so nominated in the bond? I cannot find it; 'tis
not in the bond.' "

With the temper that promptly resented these words through many newspapers of the neighboring regions there can be no propriety in wrangling. When regions so estranged from the world's thought carry their resentment no further than a little harmless invective, it is but fair to welcome it as a sign of progress. If communities nearer the great centers of thought grow impatient with *them*, how shall we resent the impatience of these remoter ones when their oldest traditions are, as it seems to them, ruthlessly assailed? There is but one right thing to do: it is to pour in upon them our reiterations of the truth without malice and without stint.

But I have a much better word to say. It is for those who, not voiced by the newspapers around them, showed both then and constantly afterward in public and private during my two days' subsequent travel and sojourn in the region, by their cordial, frequent, specific approval of my words, that a better intelligence is longing to see the evils of the old régime supplanted by a wiser and more humane public sentiment and practice. And I must repeat my conviction that if the unconscious habit of oppression were not already there, a scheme so gross, irrational, unjust, and inefficient as our present caste distinctions could not find place among a people so generally intelligent and high-minded. I ask attention to their bad influence in a direction not often noticed.

VII. THE "CONVICT LEASE SYSTEM."

In studying, about a year ago, the practice of
letting out public convicts to private lessees to
serve out their sentences under private management, I found that it does not belong to all our
once slave States nor to all our once seceded
States.[1] Only it is no longer in practice outside
of them. Under our present condition in the
South, it is beyond possibility that the individual
black should behave mischievously without offensively rearousing the old sentiments of the still
dominant white man. As we have seen too,
the white man virtually monopolizes the jury-box.
Add another fact : the Southern States have entered upon a new era of material development.
Now, if with these conditions in force the public
mind has been captivated by glowing pictures of
the remunerative economy of the convict-lease
system, and by the seductive spectacle of mines
and railways, turnpikes and levees, that everybody wants and nobody wants to pay for, growing apace by convict labor that seems to cost
nothing, we may almost assert beforehand that
the popular mind will—not so maliciously as unreflectingly—yield to the tremendous temptation
to hustle the misbehaving black man into the
State prison under extravagant sentence, and sell

[1] See " The Convict Lease System in the Southern States," in
this volume.

his labor to the highest bidder who will use him in the construction of public works. For ignorance of the awful condition of these penitentiaries is extreme and general, and the hasty half-conscious assumption naturally is, that the culprit will survive this term of sentence, and its fierce discipline " teach him to behave himself."

But we need not argue from cause to effect only. Nor need I repeat one of the many painful rumors that poured in upon me the moment I began to investigate this point. The official testimony of the prisons themselves is before the world to establish the conjectures that spring from our reasoning. After the erroneous takings of the census of 1880 in South Carolina had been corrected, the population was shown to consist of about twenty blacks to every thirteen whites. One would therefore look for a preponderance of blacks on the prison lists; and inasmuch as they are a people only twenty years ago released from servile captivity, one would not be surprised to see that preponderance large. Yet, when the actual numbers confront us, our speculations are stopped with a rude shock; for what is to account for the fact that in 1881 there were committed to the State prison at Columbia, South Carolina, 406 colored persons and but 25 whites? The proportion of blacks sentenced to the whole black population was one to every 1488; that of the whites to the white population

was but one to every 15,644. In Georgia the
white inhabitants decidedly outnumber the blacks;
yet in the State penitentiary, October 20, 1880,
there were 115 whites and 1071 colored; or if
we reject the summary of its tables and refer to
the tables themselves (for the one does not agree
with the other), there were but 102 whites and
1083 colored. Yet of 52 pardons granted in the
two years then closing, 22 were to whites and
only 30 to blacks. If this be a dark record,
what shall we say of the records of lynch law?
But for them there is not room here.

VIII. IN THE SCHOOLHOUSE.

A far pleasanter aspect of our subject shows
itself when we turn from courts and prisons
to the school-house. And the explanation is
simple. Were our educational affairs in the
hands of that not high average of the community commonly seen in jury-boxes, with their
transient sense of accountability and their crude
notions of public interests, there would most
likely be no such pleasant contrast. But with
us of the South, as elsewhere, there is a fairly
honest effort to keep the public-school interests
in the hands of the State's most highly trained
intelligence. Hence our public educational work
is a compromise between the unprogressive prejudices of the general mass of the whites and
the progressive intelligence of their best minds.

Practically, through the great majority of our higher educational officers, we are fairly converted to the imperative necessity of elevating the colored man intellectually, and are beginning to see very plainly that the whole community is sinned against in every act or attitude of oppression, however gross or however refined.

Yet one thing must be said. I believe it is wise that all have agreed not to handicap education with the race question, but to make a complete surrender of that issue, and let it find adjustment elsewhere first and in the schools last. And yet, in simple truth and justice and in the kindest spirit, we ought to file one exception for that inevitable hour when the whole question must be met. There can be no more real justice in pursuing the freedman's children with humiliating arbitrary distinctions and separations in the school-houses than in putting them upon him in other places. If, growing out of their peculiar mental structure, there are good and just reasons for their isolation, by all means let them be proved and known; but it is simply tyrannous to assume them without proof. I know that just here looms up the huge bugbear of Social Equality. Our eyes are filled with absurd visions of all Shantytown pouring its hordes of unwashed imps into the company and companionship of our own sunny-headed darlings. What utter nonsense! As if our public schools had no gauge of cleanliness,

decorum, or moral character! Social Equality!
What a godsend it would be if the advocates of
the old Southern régime could only see that the
color line points straight in the direction of social
equality by tending toward the equalization of
all whites on one side of the line and of all blacks
on the other. We may reach the moon some
day, not social equality; but the only class that
really effects anything toward it are the makers
and holders of arbitrary and artificial social distinctions interfering with society's natural self-
distribution. Even the little children everywhere
are taught, and begin to learn almost with their
A B C, that they will find, and must be guided
by, the same variations of the social scale in the
public school as out of it; and it is no small mistake to put them or their parents off their guard
by this cheap separation on the line of color.

IX. THE QUESTION OF INSTINCT.

But some will say this is not a purely artificial
distinction. We hear much about race instinct.
The most of it, I fear, is pure twaddle. It may
be there is such a thing. We do not know. It
is not proved. And even if it were established,
it would not necessarily be a proper moral guide.
We subordinate instinct to society's best interests
as apprehended in the light of reason. If there
is such a thing, it behaves with strange malignity
toward the remnants of African blood in indi-

viduals principally of our own race, and with singular indulgence to the descendants of—for example—Pocahontas. Of mere race *feeling* we all know there is no scarcity. Who is stranger to it ? And as another man's motive of private preference no one has a right to forbid it or require it. But as to its being an instinct, one thing is plain : if there is such an instinct, so far from excusing the malignant indignities practiced in its name, it furnishes their final condemnation ; for it stands to reason that just in degree as it is a real thing it will take care of itself.

It has often been seen to do so, whether it is real or imaginary. I have seen in New Orleans a Sunday-school of white children every Sunday afternoon take possession of its two rooms immediately upon their being vacated by a black school of equal or somewhat larger numbers. The teachers of the colored school are both white and black, and among the white teachers are young ladies and gentlemen of the highest social standing. The pupils of the two schools are alike neatly attired, orderly, and in every respect inoffensive to each other. I have seen the two races sitting in the same public high-school and grammar-school rooms, reciting in the same classes and taking recess on the same ground at the same time, without one particle of detriment that any one ever pretended to discover, although the fiercest enemies of the system swarmed about

it on every side.   And when in the light of these
observations I reflect upon the enormous educational task our Southern States have before them,
the inadequacy of their own means for perform-
ing it, the hoped-for beneficence of the general
Government, the sparseness with which so much
of our Southern population is distributed over
the land, the thousands of school districts where,
consequently, the multiplication of schools must
involve both increase of expense and reductions
of efficiency, I must enter some demurrer to the
enforcement of the tyrannous sentiments of the
old régime until wise experiments have established better reasons than I have yet heard given.

X. THE CASE SUBMITTED.

What need to say more?   The question is
answered.   Is the freedman a free man?   No.
We have considered his position in a land whence
nothing can, and no man has a shadow of right
to drive him, and where he is being multiplied as
only oppression can multiply a people.   We have
carefully analyzed his relations to the finer and
prouder race, with which he shares the owner-
ship and citizenship of a region large enough for
ten times the number of both.   Without accept-
ing one word of his testimony, we have shown
that the laws made for his protection against the
habits of suspicion and oppression in his late
master are being constantly set aside, not for

their defects, but for such merit as they possess. We have shown that the very natural source of these oppressions is the surviving sentiments of an extinct and now universally execrated institution; sentiments which no intelligent or moral people should harbor a moment after the admission that slavery was a moral mistake. We have shown the outrageousness of these tyrannies in some of their workings, and how distinctly they antagonize every State and national interest involved in the elevation of the colored race. Is it not well to have done so? For, I say again, the question has reached a moment of special importance. The South stands on her honor before the clean equities of the issue. It is no longer whether constitutional amendments, but whether the eternal principles of justice, are violated. And the answer must—it shall—come from the South. And it shall be practical. It will not cost much. We have had a strange experience: the withholding of simple rights has cost much blood; such concessions of them as we have made have never yet cost a drop. The answer is coming. Is politics in the way? Then let it clear the track or get run over, just as it prefers. But, as I have said over and over to my brethren in the South, I take upon me to say again here, that there is a moral and intellectual intelligence there which is not going to be much longer beguiled out of its moral right of way by questions

of political punctilio, but will seek that plane of
universal justice and equity which it is every
people's duty before God to seek, not along the
line of politics,—God forbid !—but across it and
across it and across it as many times as it may
lie across the path, until the whole people of
every once slave-holding State can stand up as
one man, saying, " Is the freedman a free man ? "
and the whole world shall answer, " Yes."

THE SILENT SOUTH

THE SILENT SOUTH.

IN Tivoli Circle, New Orleans, from the cen-
ter and apex of its green, flowery mound an
immense column of pure white marble rises in
the fair unfrowning majesty of Grecian propor-
tions high up above the city's house-tops into
the dazzling sunshine and fragrant gales of the
Delta.   On its dizzy top stands the bronze figure
of one of the world's greatest captains.

He is all alone.   Not one of his mighty lieu-
tenants stands behind or beside him or below at
the base of his pillar.   Even his horse is gone.
Only his good sword remains, hanging motion-
less in its scabbard.   His arms are folded on
that breast that never knew fear or guile, and his
calm, dauntless gaze meets the morning sun as it
rises, like the new prosperity of the land he loved
and served so masterly, above the far distant
battle-fields where so many thousands of his
ragged gray veterans lie in the sleep of fallen
heroes.

Great silent one ! who lived to see his stand-

43

ards furled and hung in the halls of the con-
queror; to hear the victor's festal jubilations; to
behold a redistribution of rights riding over the
proud traditions of his people, and all the painful fruits of a discomfited cause shaken to the
ground; to hear and see the tempestuous and
ofttimes bloody after-strife between the old ideas
and the new; to see, now on one side, now on
the other, the terms of his own grand surrender
and parole forgotten or ignored; to have his
ear filled with the tirades and recriminations of
journals and parties, and the babble of the
unthinking million; to note the old creeds
changing, and to come, himself, it may be,—God
knows,—to respect beliefs that he had once
counted follies; and yet, withal, never, before the
world that had set him aside but could not forget
him, never to quail, never to wince, never to
redden with anger, never to wail against man or
fate, or seek the salve of human praise or con-
solation; but silently amid the clamor of the
times to stand and wait, making patience royal,
with a mind too large for murmuring, and a heart
too great to break, until a Messenger as silent as
his bronze effigy beckoned Robert E. Lee to that
other land of light and flowers where man's
common inheritance of error is hidden in the
merit of his honest purpose, and lost in the
Divine charity.

So this monument, lifted far above our daily

strife of narrow interests and often narrower passions and misunderstandings, becomes a monument to more than its one great and rightly loved original. It symbolizes our whole South's better self; that finer part which the world not always sees; unaggressive, but brave, calm, thoughtful, broad-minded, dispassionate, sincere, and, in the din of boisterous error round about it, all too mute. It typifies that intelligence to which the words of a late writer most truly apply when he says concerning the long, incoherent discussion of one of our nation's most perplexing questions, "Amid it all the South has been silent."

But the times change—have changed. Whatever the merit or fault of earlier reticence, this mute, firm-rooted figure, with sheathed sword and folded arms, must yield a step, not backward, but forward. "Where it has been silent it now should speak." Nay, already it speaks; and the blessing of all good men should rest on this day if it reveals the Silent South laying off its unsurrendered sword, leaving brawlers to their brawls, and moving out upon the plane of patient, friendly debate, seeking to destroy only error, and to establish only truth and equity and a calm faith in their incomparable power to solve the dark problems of the future.

Within the last few months the voice of temperate discussion has been heard in well-nigh every quarter of our Southern States on themes that have scarcely been handled with patience and clemency these forty years. True, there has been some clamor, throwing stones, and casting dust; but calmer utterances have come from Memphis, from Louisville, Chattanooga, Lynchburg, Atlanta, Charleston, Dallas, and far San Angelo; some on one side, some on the other, of the debate, professing in common at least three quiet convictions: that recrimination and malignment of motive are the tactics of those who have no case; that the truth is worth more than any man's opinion; and that the domination of right is the end we are bound to seek.

Under these convictions the following pages are written; written in deprecation of all sectionalism; with an admiration and affection for the South, that for justice and sincerity yield to none; in a spirit of faithful sonship to a Southern State; written not to gratify sympathizers, but to persuade opponents; not to overthrow, but to convince; and begging that all harshness of fact or vehemence of statement be attributed entirely to the weight of the interests under debate.

II. POINTS OF AGREEMENT.

It is pleasant to note how much common ground is occupied by the two sides in this contest of opinions. By both it is recognized that the fate of the national Civil Rights bill has not decided and cannot dismiss the entire question of the freedman's relations ; but that it puts upon trial in each Southern State a voluntary reconstruction which can never be final till it has established the moral equities of the whole case. Says one opponent, imputing his words to a personified South, " Leave this problem to my working out. I will solve it in calmness and deliberation, without passion or prejudice, and with full regard for the unspeakable equities it holds." [1] Says Mr. Watterson's paper, in Louisville, " We believe there is a general desire among the people of the South, that the negro shall have all the rights which a citizen of the United States, whatever be the color of his skin, is entitled to, but we know of no method to argue away or force down what may be called the caste of color. If we did . . . or if anybody else did, the dark problem as to the future of this unfortunate race would be more quickly and more easily solved. None more earnestly than the *Courier-Journal* desires to see this question happily settled."

---

[1] " In Plain Black and White." April CENTURY, 1885.

Is not this progress? It seems scarce a matter of months since we were saying the question was dead and should be buried. Now it rises to demand a wider grave, which both the writers quoted admit it must have, though one thinks nobody knows how to dig it, and another insists it must be dug without cutting away any more ground.

But the common field of assertion and admission broadens as we move on. On this side it has been carefully demonstrated that, not from Emancipation or Enfranchisement, or anything else in or of the late war, or of Reconstruction, but from our earlier relation to the colored man as his master, results our view of him as naturally and irrevocably servile; and that hence arises our proneness to confuse his social with his civil relations, to argue from inferiority of race a corresponding inferiority of his rights, and to infer that they fall, therefore, justly under our own benevolent domination and, at times, even our arbitrary abridgment. The point is made that these views, as remnants of that slavery which, we all admit, has of right perished, ought to perish with it; and the fact is regretted that in many parts of the South they nevertheless still retain such force—though withal evidently weakening—that the laws affirming certain human rights discordant to the dominant race are sometimes openly evaded and sometimes virtually suf-

focated under a simulated acceptance of their
narrowest letter.   How plainly we feel the date
of this discussion to be 1884–85—not earlier—
when we hear this evasion, once so hotly denied,
admitted freely, nay, with emphasis, to be a
" matter of record, and, from the Southern
standpoint, mainly a matter of reputation."

And there are yet other points of agreement.
As one who saw our great Reconstruction agony
from its first day to its last in one of the South's
most distracted States and in its largest city, with
his sympathies ranged upon the pro-Southern
side of the issue, and his convictions drifting irresistibly to the other, the present writer affirms of
his knowledge, in the initial paper of this debate,
that after we had yielded what seemed to us all
proper deference to our slaves' emancipation and
enfranchisement, there yet remained our invinci-
ble determination—seemingly to us the fundamental condition of our self-respect—never to
yield our ancient prerogative of holding under
our own discretion the colored man's *status*, not
as a freedman, not as a voter, but in his daily walk
as a civilian.   This attitude in us, with our persistent mistaking his civil rights for social claims,
this was the tap-root of the whole trouble.   For
neither would *his* self-respect yield; and not because he was so unintelligent and base, but because he was as intelligent and aspiring as, in his
poor way, he was, did he make this the cause of

political estrangement. This estrangement—full grown at its beginning—was the carpet-bagger's and scallawag's opportunity. They spring and flourish wherever, under representative government, gentility makes a mistake, however sincere, against the rights of the poor and ignorant. Is this diagnosis of the Reconstruction malady contested by the other side? Nay, it is confirmed. The South, it tells us, "accepted the emancipation and enfranchisement of her slaves as the legitimate results of war that had been fought to a conclusion. These once accomplished, nothing more was possible. 'Thus far and no farther,' she said to her neighbors in no spirit of defiance, but with quiet determination. In her weakest moments, when her helpless people were hedged about by the unthinking bayonets of her conquerors, she gathered them for resistance at this point. Here she defended everything that a people should hold dear. There was little proclamation of her purpose," etc.

Surely hope is not folly, as to this Southern question, when such admissions come from this direction. What salutary clearing of the ground have we here! Our common assertion in the South has long been that the base governments of the Reconstruction period were overturned by force because they had become so corrupt that they were nothing but huge machines for the robbery of the whole public, a tangle of low po-

litical intrigues that no human intelligence could
unravel; that our virtue and intelligence sought
not the abridgment of any man's rights, but
simply the arrest of bribery and robbery; that
this could be done only by revolution because
of the solid black vote, cast, we said, without rationality at the behest of a few scoundrels who
kept it solid by playing upon partisan catch-
words, or by promise of spoils. And especially
among those whose faith is strongest in our old
Southern traditions, it always was and is, to-day,
sincerely believed that this was the whole issue.
It was this profession that averted the interference of Federal arms. It was upon this profession that the manliest youth and intelligence
of New Orleans went forth to stake their lives,
and some to pour out their hearts' blood in inter-
necine war on the levee of their dear city. Sad
sight to those who knew that this was *not* the
whole matter—that the spring of trouble lay yet
deeper down. To such it brings no small or
selfish gladness to hear, at length,—if one may
without offence coin a term,—to hear Southern
traditionists admitting a truth which the South
has denied with sincere indignation ten thousand
times,—that in all that terrible era the real, fundamental issue was something else which the
popular Southern mind was hardly aware of.
"Barely"—say these—"barely did the whispered
word that bespoke her [the South's] resolution

catch the listening ears of her sons; but for all
this, the victorious armies of the North, had they
been rallied again from their homes, could not have
enforced and maintained among this disarmed
people the policy indicated in the Civil Rights bill."
This was the point at which, they say, and they say
truly, the South "gathered for resistance."

Let us be sure these so gallantly spoken words
are not misunderstood. There were two policies
indicated in the Civil Rights bill : the policy of
asserting congressional jurisdiction in the case;
and the policy of legalizing, at all, such rights as
it declared. One raised a question of State
rights; the other, of Human rights. But the
State-rights issue, by itself,—the mere question
of whence the legislation should emanate, could
never of itself make fierce strife. Any State
could have settled that point by simply stepping
ahead of Congress with the same legislation.
No ; the irreconcilable difference was not as to
whence but as to *what* the law should be. The
essential odium of the bill lay not in its origin, but
in its definition of the black man's rights. Indeed, the main object of most of those who have
written on the other side in the present controversy has been to assert the resolution never to
recognize the freedman's rights upon that definition of them. In the meantime a gentle movement of thought, that sounds no trumpet before it,
is gradually pressing toward that very recognition.

III. THE STICKING POINT.

But now that we have clearly made out exactly *what* this immovable hostility is, the question follows—and half the nation are asking it to-day with perplexed brows—*why* is it? Yet the answer is simple. Many white people of the South sincerely believe that the recognition of rights proposed in the old Civil Rights bills or in "The Freedman's Case in Equity" *would precipitate a social chaos.* They believe Civil Rights means Social Equality. This may seem a transparent error, but certainly any community in the world that believed it, would hold the two ideas in equal abomination; and it is because of the total unconsciousness and intense activity of this error at the South, and the subtle sense of unsafety that naturally accompanies it,—it is because of this, rather than for any lack of clearness in its statement of the subject, that the article on "The Freedman's Case in Equity" is so grossly misinterpreted even by some who undoubtedly wish to be fair. That this is the true cause of the misinterpretation is clear in the fact that from the first printing of the article until now the misconstruction has occurred only among those whose thinking still runs in the grooves of the old traditions.

Nothing in that paper touches or seeks to touch the domain of social privileges. The standing of the magazine in which it appears is guarantee against the possibility of the paper containing any such insult to the intelligence of enlightened society. Social equality is a fool's dream. The present writer wants quite as little of it as the most fervent traditionist of the most fervent South. The North, the West, the East, and the rest of the intelligent world, want quite as little of it as the South wants. Social equality can never exist where a community, numerous enough to assert itself, is actuated, as every civilized community is, by an intellectual and moral ambition. No form of laws, no definition of rights, from Anarchy to Utopia, can bring it about. The fear that this or that change will produce it ought never to be any but a fool's fear. And yet there is this to be added; that no other people in America are doing so much *for* social equality as those who, while they warmly charge it upon others, are themselves thrusting arbitrary and cheap artificial distinctions into the delicate machinery of society's self-distribution as it revolves by the power of our natural impulses, and of morality, personal interest, and personal preferences. This, of course, is not the intention, and even these persons retard only incidentally, unawares and within narrow limits, nature's social distributions, while taking diligent and absolutely needless pains to hold apart two races which really have no social affinity at all.

Do we charge any bad intention or conscious false pretense? Not at all! They are merely making the double mistake of first classing as personal social privileges certain common impersonal rights of man, and then turning about and treating them as rights definable by law—which social amenities are not and cannot be.

For the sake of any who might still misunderstand, let us enlarge here a moment. The family relation has *rights.* Hence marital laws and laws of succession. But beyond the family circle there are no such things as social *rights;* and when our traditionists talk about a too hasty sympathy having " fixed by enactment " the negro's *social* and civil rights they talk—unwisely. All the relations of life that go by *impersonal right* are Civil relations. All that go by *personal choice* are Social relations. The one is all of right, it makes no difference who we are ; the other is all of choice, and it makes all the difference who we are ; and it is no little fault against ourselves as well as others, to make confusion between the two relations. For the one we make laws ; for the other every one consults his own pleasure ; and the law that refuses to protect a civil right, construing it a social privilege, deserves no more regard than if it should declare some social privilege to be a civil right. Social *choice*, civil *rights;* but a civil *privilege*, in America, is simply heresy against both our great

national political parties at once. Now, "The
Freedman's Case in Equity" pleads for not one
thing belonging to the domain of social relations.   Much less the family relation; it does
not hint the faintest approval of any sort of
admixture of the two bloods.   Surely nothing
that a man can buy a ticket for anonymously at
a ticket-seller's hand-hole confers the faintest
right to even a bow of recognition that any one
may choose to withhold.   But what says the
other side?   "The South will never adopt the
suggestion of the *social intermingling*[1] of the two
races."   So they beg the question of equity, and
suppress a question of civil right by simply mis-
calling it "social intermingling"; thus claiming
for it that sacredness from even the law's control
which only social relations have, and the next
instant asserting the determination of one race
to "control the social relations," so-called, of two.
Did ever champions of a cause with blanker simplicity walk into a sack and sew up its mouth?
Not only thus, but from within it they announce
a doctrine that neither political party in our
country would venture to maintain ; for no party
dare say that in these United States there is
any room for any one class of citizens to fasten
arbitrarily upon any other class of citizens a *civil
status* from which no merit of intelligence, virtue,
or possessions can earn an extrication.· We have

[1] Italicized only here.

a country large enough for all the *unsociality* anybody may want, but not for *incivility* either by or
without the warrant of law.

"What history shows," says a sound little
book lately printed, " is that rights are safe only
when guaranteed against all arbitrary power and
all class and personal interest." Class rule of
any sort is bad enough, even with the consent of
the ruled class; un-American enough. But the
domination of one fixed class by another without
its consent, is Asiatic. And yet it is behind this
error, of Asian antiquity and tyranny, this arbitrary suppression of impartial, impersonal civil
rights, that we discover our intelligent adver-
saries in this debate fortified, imagining they have
found a strong position! " Neither race wants
it," says one; alluding to that common, undivided participation in the enjoyment of civil
rights, for which the darker race has been lifting
one long prayer these twenty years, and which
he absurdly miscalls " social intermingling."
" The interest, as the inclination, of both races is
against it," he adds. " Here the issue is made
up."

But he mistakes. The issue is not made up
here at all. It is not a question of what the *race*
wants, but of *what the individual wants and has
a right to.* Is that question met? No. Not a
line has been written to disprove the individual
freedman's title to these rights; but pages, to

declare that his *race* does not want them and
shall not have them if it does. Mark the contra-
diction.   It does not want them—it shall not
have them! Argument unworthy of the nursery;
yet the final essence of all the other side's utterances.   They say the colored race wants a participation in public rights separate from the
whites; and that anyhow it has got to take that
or nothing; " The white and black races in the
South *must*[1] walk apart." One writer justifies
this on the belief of a natal race instinct; but
says that if there were no such thing the South
"would, by every means in its power, so strengthen
the race *prejudice*[1] that it would do the work and
hold the stubbornness and strength of instinct."
Could any one more distinctly or unconsciously
waive the whole question of right and wrong?
Yet this is the standpoint on which it is proposed
to meet the freedmen's case *in equity*.   Under the
heat of such utterances how the substance melts
out of their writer's later proposition for the
South to solve the question " without passion or
prejudice and with full regard for the unspeakable equities it holds."

It is not the Louisville gentlemen who are
found at this untenable standpoint.   They admit
the desirability of extirpating the state of affairs
condemned by "The Freedman's Case in Equity,"
and merely ask with a smile, " in what manner

[1] Italicized only here.

the writer expects that evil to disappear before
high-sounding imperatives," etc.   As to that we
leave others on that side to give the answer;
hear it, from Atlanta: " Clear views, clear statement, and clear understanding are the demands
of the hour.   Given these, the common sense
and courage of the American people will make
the rest easy."

IV. CIVIL RIGHT NOT SOCIAL CHOICE.

Let us then make our conception of the right
and wrong of this matter unmistakable.   Social
relations, one will say, are sacred.   True, but
civil rights are sacred, also.   Hence social relations must not impose upon civil rights nor civil
rights impose upon social relations.   We must
have peace.   But for peace to be stable we must
have justice.   Therefore, for peace, we must find
that boundary line between social relations and
civil rights, from which the one has no warrant
ever to push the other; and, for justice, this
boundary must remain ever faithfully the same,
no matter whose the social relations are on one
side or whose the civil rights are on the other.

Suppose a case.   Mr. A. takes a lady, not of
his own family, to a concert.   Neither one is
moved by compulsion or any assertion of right
on the part of the other.   They have chosen
each other's company.   Their relation is social.
It could not exist without mutual agreement.

They are strangers in that city, however, and as they sit in the thronged auditorium and look around them, not one other soul in that house, so far as they can discern, has any social relation with them. But see, now, how impregnable the social relation is. That pair, outnumbered a thousand to one, need not yield a pennyweight of social interchange with any third person unless they so choose. Nothing else in human life is so amply sufficient to protect itself as are social relations. Provided one thing,—that the law will protect every one impartially in his civil rights, one of the foremost of which is that both men and laws shall let us alone to our personal social preferences. If any person, no matter who or what he is, insists on obtruding himself upon this pair in the concert-hall he can only succeed in getting himself put out. Why? Because he is trying to turn his civil right-to-be-there into a social passport. And even if he make no personal advances, but his behavior or personal condition is so bad as to obtrude itself offensively upon others, the case is the same; the mistake and its consequences are his. But, on the other hand, should Mr. A. and his companion demand the expulsion of this third person when he had made no advances and had encroached no more on their liberty than they had on his, demanding it simply on the ground that he was their social or intellectual inferior or probably had relatives

who were, then the error, no matter who or what
he is, would be not his, but theirs, and it would
be the equally ungenteel error of trying to turn
their social choice into a civil right; and it would
be simply increasing the error and its offensive-
ness, for them to suggest that he be given an
equally comfortable place elsewhere in the house
providing it must indicate his inferiority. There
is nothing comfortable in ignominy, nor is it any
evidence of high mind for one stranger to put it
upon another.

Now, the principles of this case are not dis-
turbed by any multiplication of the number of
persons concerned, or by reading for concert-
hall either theatre or steamboat or railway station
or coach or lecture-hall or street car or public
library, or by supposing the social pair to be
English, Turk, Jap, Cherokee, Ethiopian, Mexi-
can, or " American." But note the fact that,
even so, Mr. A. and his companion's social relations are, under these rulings, as safe from inva-
sion as they were before; nay, even safer, inasmuch as the true distinction is made publicly
clearer, between the social and the civil relations.
Mr. A. is just as free to decline every sort of
unwelcome social advance, much or little, as ever
he was ; and as to his own house or estate may
eject any one from it, not of his own family or a
legal tenant, and give no other reason than that
it suits him to do so. Do you not see it now,

gentlemen of the other side? Is there anything new in it? Is it not as old as truth itself? Honestly, have you not known it all along? Is it not actually the part of good breeding to know it? You cannot say no. Then why have you charged us with proposing "to break down every distinction between the races," and "to insist on their intermingling in all places and in all relations," when in fact we have not proposed to disturb any distinction between the races which nature has made, or molest any private or personal relation in life, whatever? Why have you charged us with "moving to forbid all further assortment of the races," when the utmost we have done is to condemn an *arbitrary* assortment of the races, crude and unreasonable, by the stronger race without the consent of the weaker, and in places and relations where no one, exalted or lowly, has any right to dictate to another because of the class he belongs to? We but turn your own words to our use when we say this battery of charges " is as false as it is infamous." But let that go.

Having made it plain that the question has nothing to do with social relations, we see that it is, and is only, a question of *indiscriminative civil rights*. This is what " The Freedman's Case in Equity " advocates from beginning to end, not as a choice which a *race* may either claim or disclaim, but as every citizen's individual yet im-

personal right until he personally waives or for-
feits it. The issue, we repeat, is not met at all
by the assertion that " Neither race wants it."
There is one thing that neither race wants, but
even this is not because either of them is one
race or another, but simply because they are
members of a civilized human community. It is
that thing of which our Southern white people
have so long had such an absurd fear; neither
race, or in other words nobody, wants to see the
civil rewards of decency in dress and behavior
usurped by the common herd of clowns and
ragamuffins. But there is another thing that the
colored race certainly does want : the freedom
for those of the race who can to earn the indiscriminative and unchallenged *civil—not social—*
rights of gentility by the simple act of being
genteel. This is what we insist the best intelligence of the South is willing—in the interest
of right, and therefore of both races—to accord.
But the best intelligence is not the majority, and
the majority, leaning not upon the equities, but
the traditional sentiments of the situation, charge
us with " theory " and "sentiment" and give us
their word for it that " Neither race wants it."

Why, that is the very same thing we used to
say about slavery ! Where have these traditionists
been the last twenty years ? Who, that lived in
the South through those days, but knows that
the darker race's demand from the first day of

the Reconstruction era to its last, was, "If you
will not give us undivided participation in civil
rights, *then and in that case* you must give us
equal separate enjoyment of them"; and from
the close of Reconstruction to this day the only
change in its expression has been to turn its imperative demand into a supplication.   This was
the demand, this is the supplication of American
citizens seeking not even their civil rights entire,
but their civil rights mutilated to accommodate
not our public rights but our private tastes.
And how have we responded ? Has the separate
accommodation furnished them been anywhere
nearly equal to ours ?   Not one time in a thousand.   Has this been for malice ?   Certainly not.
But we have unconsciously—and what people in
our position would not have made the same oversight ?—allowed ourselves to be carried off the
lines of even justice by our old notion of every
white man holding every negro to a menial
status.

   Would our friends on the other side of the discussion say they mean only, concerning these
indiscriminative civil rights, " Neither race wants
them *now* " ? This would but make bad worse.
For two new things have happened to the colored race in these twenty years; first, a natural
and spontaneous assortment has taken place
within the race itself along scales of virtue and
intelligence, knowledge and manners; so that by

no small fraction of their number the wrong of
treating the whole race alike is more acutely felt
than ever it was before; and, second, a long, bit-
ter experience has taught them that "equal
accommodations, but separate" means, generally,
accommodations of a conspicuously ignominious
inferiority. Are these people opposed to an
arrangement that would give them instant re-
lease from organized and legalized incivility?—
For that is what a race distinction in civil relations is when it ignores intelligence and decorum.

V. CALLING THE WITNESSES.

There is another way to settle this question
of fact. One side in this debate advocates indiscriminative civil rights; the other, separate—
racial civil rights. It is not to be doubted that
our opponents have received many letters from
white men and women full of commendation and
thanks for what they have written. Such, too,
has been the present writer's experience. Such
testimonials poured in upon him daily for four
months, from east, west, north, and south. But
how about the colored race? Have they written
him, begging him to desist because "Neither
race wants" the equities he pleads for? The
pages of this essay are limited, but we beg
room for a few extracts from colored correspond-
ents' letters, each being from a separate letter and
no letter from any colored person whom the pres-

ent writer has ever seen or known. One letter ends,
" May all the spirits that aid justice, truth, and
right constantly attend you in your effort." Another, " I hope that you will continue the work
you have begun, and may God bless you." Another, "Accept this, dear sir, as the thanks of the
colored people of this city." Another begins,
" I am a negro. In behalf of the negroes and in
behalf of equitable fair dealing on the principle of giving a dollar's worth for a dollar, without any possible reference to social matters, permit me to tender you my sincere thanks," etc.
Says another, " The judicious fairness with which
you have treated our case renders your thesis
worthy of our adoption as a Bill of Rights." A
letter of thanks from a colored literary club
says, ". . . We thank you for your recognition
of our capacity to suffer keenly under the indignities we are made to endure." A similar society
in another town sent a verbal expression of
thanks by its president in person. (Followed
since by its committee's formal resolution orna-
mentally written and mounted.) In Louisville
a numerous impromptu delegation of colored
citizens called upon the writer and tendered a
verbal address of thanks. Another letter says,
"If the people of the South will only regard
your article in the same spirit as I believe it
was intended, then I know, sir, great and enduring good will be accomplished." In Arkansas,

a meeting of colored people, called to express approval of the article on " The Freedman's Case in Equity," passed a resolution pronouncing its ideas " consonant with true religion and enlightened civilization," etc. Not one word of adverse criticism, written or printed, has come to him from a person of color. Has the same race given " In Plain Black and White," or " The Freedman's Case in Reality," or any of the less dignified mass of matter on that side of the question, a like cordial ratification ? Or has only Mr. Jack Brown sent in his congratulation ? [1]

---

[1] The Selma " Times," quoted in " The Freedman's Case in Equity " as rejoicing in the flogging of a colored preacher on a railway train for not leaving the passenger coach when ordered out by irresponsible ruffians, has since published a letter purporting to come from one " Jack Brown, colored," of Columbia, South Carolina.   The letter denounces the present writer as one of the sort " that has brought on all the trouble between the white and colored people of the South.   I do not know his initials or address," it continues, " or I would address him in person, as I am anxious to *test his sincerity*." † " Now," says the Selma " Times," " the above article bears every imprint of honesty and truthfulness.   We don't believe any one but a sharp negro could have written or did write it.   The handwriting, the loose grammar, the postmark on the envelope, all mark it as a genuine document coming from the man it purports to have come from.   Not only is this true of such external marks as we have named, but so is it likewise of its internal, essential substance.   It sounds as if it could have been thought out and written by a negro *only*.

† So italicized originally.

But it may be asked, may not a great many individuals, and even some clubs, impromptu delegations and public meetings called for the purpose, approve certain declarations and yet the great mass of a people not sanction them ? Then let us go one step farther.   There are, it is said, eighty—some say a hundred—journals published in this country by colored men.   They look to

We cannot conceive of a white man's putting himself so thoroughly into the place of a negro, mentally, as to have executed such a thing as a forgery. We shall find out if there is such a negro in Columbia, S. C., as Brown, and secure other proofs that he wrote it, because we know Mr. Cable and others are sure to challenge its authenticity. We confidently expect to be fully prepared to convince the most skeptical.

" The negro is right. Those of his race who have any sense cannot expect what Mr. Cable would give them, do not expect it, and would be unhappy and uncomfortable if, in any way, it could be forced upon them."

So if Jack Brown, colored, were a real person, nothing could be easier than to find him. Writing from a small inland city, getting through one hundred and seventy-five words of his letter before making a grammatical slip, a colored man in sympathy with the tritest sentiment of the dominant race, and with a taste for public questions,—such a man could not be hid, much less overlooked, in Columbia.   But on the present writer's desk lies his own letter *to* Mr. Jack Brown, colored, stamped " Return to the writer," after having lain in the Columbia post-office for nearly a month, unclaimed.   An exhaustive search and inquiry amongst the people of both races by a white gentleman resident on the spot, fails to find any " Jack Brown " except—to quote the gentleman's letter,—" a poor, illiterate fellow, who cannot read or write his name," and who, instead of being "twenty-seven years of age," is—to quote another letter—" an aged man."

the colored race for the great bulk of their
readers and subscribers.   Hence they are bound
to be in large degree the organs of popular
thought among the reading part, at least, of that
people.   But *these papers are a unit for the ideas
set forth in " The Freedman's Case in Equity."*
Now, to believe the other side we should have to
make two impossible assumptions ; that among a
people treated rigorously as one race, compacted
by a common status, the intelligent and comparatively refined part numerous enough to send
—in spite of its poverty—*twenty thousand students
to normal schools and colleges* and to support
eighty newspapers, this portion, moreover, asso-
ciated with the less intelligent portion more
cordially in every interest than two such classes
are amongst any other people in the world unless
it be the Jews—that such a lump of leaven as
this has no power to shape the views of the
rest on matters of common public right !   Such
a thing may be credible on some other planet,
not on this.   And the second impossible assumption : That the intelligent and sensitive portions
of a people shall submit to an ignominious mutilation of their public rights because the *unintelligence* of their race chooses (?) to submit to it.
This assumption is a crime against common
justice ; the other is a crime against common
sense.   It is simply a mistake that " the assortment of the races which has been described

as shameful and unjust . . . commands the
hearty assent of both."

True, our traditionist friends, who think they
believe it, are glad to take the witness-stand and
testify; but surely some of them should be law-
yer enough to know that when they say the colored race *shall not have* the other thing in any
event, their testimony as to which the colored
race prefers is of no further account.   At Atlanta,
they are equally unfortunate in another witness.
If the Georgia State Commissioner of Public
Education will allow the personal mention from
one who has met and admires him, we may say
that throughout the United States he has won the
high regard and praise of the friends of public
education for the exceptional progress he—a man
of the old South—has made in unlearning our
traditional Southern prejudices. He stands a
noble, personal refutation of the superficial notion
that the world must look to the young South,
only, for progressive ideas of human right among
us.   May be it was easy to make the mistake of
calling this admirable gentleman to testify that
" neither race wants it."   But see how quickly
Commissioner Orr provokes the reader to dismiss him, too, from the witness-stand : Speaking
of mixed schools, which, he says, " both races
would protest against "—but which, mark it,
"The Freedman's Case in Equity " does not ask
to have forced upon any community or forced

by either race upon the other anywhere—Mr. Orr says, " I am so sure of the evils that would come from mixed schools that, even if they were possible, I would see the whole educational system swept away before I would see them established."

Ah! gentlemen, you are not before a Congressional investigating committee that gets Republican facts from Republican witnesses and Democratic facts from Democratic witnesses, and then makes two reports. You are before the judgment-seat of the world's intelligence; and if you cannot bring for evidence of a people's feelings their own spontaneous and habitual expressions to those who think with them; and, for the establishment of facts, the unconscious or unwilling testimony of your opponents, then it is high time you were taking your case out of this court.[1] As for us we can prove all we need prove by the gentlemen themselves.

[1] They might easily have brought in colored school teachers. Many of these favor separate colored schools, for the obvious reason that those are the only schools they may teach in. They do bring in just two witnesses from a side avowedly opposed to them; but it is not our side, either. One is the late Bishop Haven, of whom we shall speak presently. The other, a young white woman on a railway train, who—forbidden to enjoy her civil rights and her peculiar social preferences at the same time— threw away a civil right to retain the social preference; which was her business, not ours, and proves nothing whatever for or against anybody else; but whose expression of *pride* at being mistaken for a quadroon proves her an extremely silly person.

Once only does the opposite side bring forward the actual free utterance of a colored man
professing to express a sentiment of his race;
well nigh a magazine column of "negro elo-
quence" and adulation poured upon a conference of applauding "Bishops and Brethren"
because of the amazing fact that when in the
neighboring vestry-room, he had "thoughtlessly
asked" the governor of the State if he could get
a drink, that magnate sent for and handed him a
glass of water! Unlucky testimony! which no
candid mind can deny is an elaborate confession
of surprised delight at being treated with indiscriminative civility. We are told, however, that
it is offered simply to show the affectionate "feeling of that people toward their white neighbors."
Thus a display of affection is utilized to give a
color of justice to the *mutilation* of just such
equal rights as this one whose unexpected recognition called forth this display of affection! So
they go round and round their tether.

They summon her for "the sole object" of suggesting that she
and such as agree with her—which lets us out as plainly as it
does the other side—are "unsafe as advisers and unfair as witnesses." Certainly they are.

VI. GUNS THAT SHOOT BACKWARD.

Our demonstration is complete; but there follows a short corollary: While the colored people always did and still do accept with alacrity an undivided enjoyment of civil rights with the white race wherever cordially offered, they never mistake them for social privileges, nor do they ever attempt to use them to compel social intercourse. We might appeal to the everyday street-car experience of hundreds of thousands of residents in New Orleans and other Southern cities; or to the uniform clearness with which civil rights are claimed and social advances disclaimed in the many letters from colored men and women that are this moment before the writer. But we need not. We need refer only to our opponents in debate, who bring forward, to prove their own propositions, a set of well-known facts that turn and play Balaam to their Balak. Hear their statement: "They"—the colored people—"meet the white people in all the avenues of business. They work side by side with the white bricklayer or carpenter in perfect accord and friendliness. When the trowel or hammer is laid aside, the laborers part, each going his own way. Any attempt to carry the comradeship of the day into private life would be sternly resisted by both parties in interest."

We prove, by the other side's own arguments,

that the colored people always accept the common enjoyment of civil rights and never confound civil with social relations.   But in just one phase of life there is a conspicuous exception; and an exception especially damaging to the traditional arguments of our opponents.   And who furnishes our evidence this time?   Themselves again.   We allude to the church relation.   We are asked to confront the history of an effort made, they say, many times over, by Bishop Haven and the Northern Methodist church generally, soon after the late war; an effort to abolish racial discrimination in the religious worship of the church in the South composed of Northern whites and Southern blacks; its constant and utter failure; and the final separation of those churches into two separate conferences, and into separate congregations wherever practicable. These facts are brought forward to prove the existence of race instinct, intending to justify by race instinct the arbitrary control, by the whites of the relations between the two races; and the conclusion is sanguinely reached at a bound, that the only explanation of these churches' separation on the color line is each race's race instinct, "that spoke above the appeal of the bishop and dominated the divine influences that pulsed from pew to pew."   But the gentlemen are too eager. What in their haste they omit to do is to make any serious search at all for a simpler explana-

tion.   And how simple the true explanation is !
Bishop Haven and his colleagues, if rightly reported, ought to have known they would fail.
They were attempting under acute disadvantages
what none of the Protestant churches in America,
faithfully as they have striven for it, has ever been
able extensively to accomplish.   That is, *to get
high and low life to worship together.*   The character of much ritual worship and of nearly all
non-ritual worship naturally and properly takes
for its standard the congregation's average intelligence.   But this good process of assortment,
unless held in by every proper drawback, flies
off to an excess that leaves the simple and unlearned to a spiritual starvation apparently as bad
as that from which non-ritual worship, especially,
professes to revolt. Bishop Dudley, of Kentucky,
has lately laid his finger upon this mischief for
us with great emphasis.   But, moreover, as in
society, so in the church, this intellectual standard
easily degenerates toward a standard of mere
manners or station.   Thus the gate is thrown
wide open to the social idea, and presently not
our Dorcases only, but at times our very bishops
and elders, are busy trying to make the social
relation co-extensive with the church relation.
With what result ?   Little, generally, save the
bad result of congregations trimming themselves
down to fit the limitations of social fellowship.
See the case cited.   Here were whites, cultured,

and counting themselves, at least, as good as the best in the land; and here was an ignorant, superstitious race of boisterous worshipers just emerged from slavery; one side craving spiritual meat, the other needing spiritual milk, and both sides beset by our prevalent American error that social intimacy is one of the distinct *earnings* of church membership. Of course they separated.

It is but a dwarfed idea of the church relation that cramps it into the social relation. The church relation is the grandest fraternity on earth.[1] Social relations are good and proper, but can the social relation grasp all these conditions in one embrace? Can any one social circle span from the drawing-room to the stable, from the counting-room or professional desk to the kitchen, from the judge's bench to the tailor's and cobbler's, from the prince's crown to the pauper's bowl? Yet without any social intimacy the prince may be the pauper's best friend, and even the pauper the prince's; and the church relation ought to be so wide and high that all these ranks might kneel abreast in it in common worship, and move abreast in it in perfect, active, colaboring fraternity and regard, gathering any or every social circle into its noble circumference, never pressing one injuriously upon another, and above all things never letting in the slender but

[1] " There is neither Jew nor Greek, there is neither bond nor free, there is neither male nor female." Gal. iii. 28.

mischievous error of confusing Christian fraternity with social equality. Yet the high and
low nigh all our country over are kept apart in
divine worship by just this error or the fear of it.
Fifty thousand Bishop Haven's could not, until
they had overthrown the domination of this mistake, get the lofty and the lowly to worship together. How could they but separate? And
the dragging in of a race instinct to account for
the separation is like bringing a pole to knock
down strawberries. Other things *will*, but a belief in instinct will *not*, keep the races apart.
Look at the West Indies. But not even miscegenation—may the reader forgive us the be-
draggled word—could have saved such a scheme
from failure.

The gentlemen prove absolutely nothing for
their case, but much against it. For here is
shown by actual experiment that even where
there is not of necessity a social relation, yet
when the social idea merely gets in by mistake
of both classes, the effect will not be social confusion, but a spontaneous and willing separation
along the strongest lines of social cleavage. The
log—the church—will not split the wedge—the
social impulse; but the wedge will split the log.
The uncultured, be they white or black, in North
or South, will break away on one side with even
more promptness and spontaneity than the cultured on the other, and will recoil, moreover, to

a greater distance than is best for any one concerned. Thus far are we from having the least ground to fear from the blacks that emptiest of phantasms, social aggression. Thus far are we from needing for the protection of social order any assumption of race instinct. And so do the advocates of our traditional sentiments continually establish the opposite of what they seek to prove.

They cite, again, to establish this assumption of race instinct, the spontaneous grouping together of colored people in such social or semi-social organizations as Masonic lodges, military companies, etc. But there is no proscription of whites in the lodges of colored Odd-fellows or Masons. In Georgia, for example, the *law requires* the separation of the races in military companies. The gentlemen forget that the colored people are subject to a strong expulsive power from the whites, which they say must and shall continue whether it is instinct or not; and that the existence of a race instinct can never be proved or disproved until all expulsive forces are withdrawn and both races are left totally free to the influences of those entirely self-sufficient *social* forces which one of the gentlemen has so neatly termed " centripetal." But even if these overlooked facts were out of existence, what would be proved? Only, and for the second time, that the centripetal force of social selection operates

so completely to the fulfillment of these gentlemen's wishes, that there is no longer any call to
prove or disprove the existence of race instinct,
or the faintest excuse for arbitrary race separations in the enjoyment of civil rights.

Thus, setting out with the idea that the social
integrity of the races requires vigorous protection
from without, they prove instead by every argument brought to establish it, that every relation
really social, partially social, or even mistakenly
social, takes—instinct or no instinct—the most
spontaneous and complete care of itself. We
are debating the freedman's title to a totally impersonal freedom in the enjoyment of all impersonal rights ; and they succeed only in *saying*,
never in bringing a particle of legitimate evidence
to prove, that " Neither race wants it " ; an assertion which no sane man, knowing the facts,
can sincerely make until, like these gentlemen,
he has first made the most woful confusion in
his own mind between personal social privileges
and impersonal civil rights.

VII. THE RIGHT TO RULE.

But they have yet one last fancied stronghold.
They say, " The *interest* of both races is against
it " ; that is, against a common participation in
their civil rights ; and that it is, rather, in favor of
a separate enjoyment of them. Now, there are
people—but their number is steadily growing less

—who would mean by this merely that the interest of both races is against common participation because *they* are against it and have made separate participation the price of peace. But the gentlemen whom we have in view in these chapters, though they must confess their lines often imply this, give a reason somewhat less offensive in its intention. They say common participation means common sociality, and common sociality, race-amalgamation. Have we not just used their own facts to show conclusively that this is not what occurs? Yet these two reasons, so called, are actually the only ones that scrutiny can find in all the utterances pledging these gentlemen to " the exactest justice and the fullest equity." Nay, there is another; we must maintain, they say, " the clear and unmistakable domination of the white race in the South."— Why, certainly we must! and we must do it honestly and without tampering with anybody's natural rights ; and we can do it! But why do *they* say we must do it? Because " character, intelligence, and property " belong preëminently to the white race, and " character, intelligence, and property " have " the right to rule." So, as far as the reasoning is sincere, they are bound to mean that not merely being white entails this right, but the possession of " character, intelligence, and property." And the true formula becomes " the clear and unmistakable

domination " of " character, intelligence, and
property " " in the South." But if this be the
true doctrine, as who can deny it is ? then why
—after we have run the color line to suit ourselves through all our truly social relations—
why need we usurp the prerogative to run it so
needlessly through civil rights, also ? It is
widely admitted that we are vastly the superior
race in everything—as a race. But is every colored man inferior to every white man in character, intelligence, and property ? Is there no " responsible and steadfast element " at all among a
people who furnish 16,000 school-teachers and
are assessed for $91,000,000 worth of taxable
property ? Are there no poor and irresponsible whites ? So, the color line and the line of
character, intelligence, and property frequently
cross each other. Then tell us, gentlemen,
which are you really for ; the color line, or the
line of character, intelligence, and property that
divides between those who have and those who
have not " the right to rule " ? You dare not
declare for an inflexible color line ; such an answer would shame the political intelligence of a
Russian.

Another point just here. The right to rule :
What is it ? It is not the right to take any
peaceable citizen's civil right from him in whole
or in part. It is not the right to decree who may
earn or not earn any *status* within the reach of

his proper powers. It is not the right to oppress. In America, to rule is to serve. There is a newspaper published in Atlanta called " The Constitution." The Instrument of which this name is intended to remind us, and of which it is well to keep us reminded, is founded on a simple principle that solves the problem of free government over which Europe sat in dark perplexity for centuries, shedding tears of blood; the principle that the right to rule is the consent of the ruled and is vested in the majority by the consent of all. It took ages of agony for the human race to discover that there is no moral right of class rule, and that the only safety to human freedom lies in the intelligence, virtue, and wealth of communities holding every right of every being in such sacred regard, and all claims for class or personal privilege in such uniform contempt, that unintelligence, vice, and poverty, having no potent common grievance, shall naturally invest intelligence, character, and property with the right to rule. It took ages for us to discover the necessity of binding intelligence, character, and property to the maintenance of this attitude by giving, once for all, to the *majority* the custody and right-of-assignment of this truly precious right to rule. Is this mere sentiment? A scheme in the clouds? Who says so cannot truly qualify as a whole American citizen. The safety of American government is that intelligence, virtue, and wealth

dare not press any measure whose viciousness or
tyranny might suspend the expulsive forces that
keep unintelligence, vice, and poverty divided
among themselves ; and that intelligence and
virtue hold themselves entirely free to combine
now with wealth and now with poverty as now
the lower million or now the upper ten shows the
livelier disposition to impose upon the other.
But the only way to preserve these conditions is
to hold sacred the will and voice of the majority.
Of course there are friction and imperfections in
their working ; but human wisdom has not yet
found any other scheme that carries us so near
to perfect government. The right to rule is a
right to earn the confidence and choice of the
majority of the whole unfettered people. Yet it
is in the face of this fundamental principle of
American freedom that our traditionist friends
stand, compelling six million freedmen to mass
together under a group of common grievances,
within a wall of these gentlemen's own avowed
building, then charging them with being
" leagued together in ignorance and irresponsibility," and then talking in large approval about
" *minorities* "—not earning, but—" *asserting and
maintaining* control." And a proposition to set
such antique usurpation of human rights aside,
to remove the real grievances that make a common cause for six million distrusted and distrust-
ing people, to pull down that wall of civil—*not*

social—distinctions that tends to keep them
" leagued together in ignorance and irresponsibility," to open to them the *civil*—not social—
rewards of gentility and education, and the responsibilities of knowledge and citizenship, to
arouse in them the same concern in common public interests that we feel, and to make all their fortunes subject to the same influences as ours,—
this, we are told, is " against the interest of both
races " !   And this we have from men who,
claiming a preëminent right to speak for the
South, claim with it a " right to rule " that fails to
signify anything better than the right of the white
man to rule the black without his consent and
without any further discrimination between intelligence and unintelligence or between responsibility and irresponsibility.   In other words, a
principle of political and civil selection such as
no freeman could possibly choose and which cannot be the best interest of any American community.   So the other side are our witnesses
again.   And now we may say to them, as the
lawyers do in court,—" That will do."

VIII. SUMMING UP.

The case is before the reader.   The points of
fact made in our earlier paper—the privations
suffered by the colored people in their matters of civil rights—have been met with feeble
half-denials equivalent to admissions by oppo-

nents in controversy too engrossed with counter statements and arguments, that crumble at the touch, to attend to a statement of facts.   In the end they stand thus : As to churches, there is probably not a dozen in the land, if one, " colored " or " white," where a white person is not at least professedly welcome to its best accommodations ; while the colored man, though he be seven-eighths white, is shut up, on the ground that " his race " prefers it, to the poor and often unprofitable appointments of the " African " church, whether he like it best or not, unless he is ready to accept without a murmur distinctions that mark him, in the sight of the whole people, as one of a despised caste and that follow him through the very sacraments.   As to schooling, despite the fact that he is to-day showing his eager willingness to accept separate schools for his children wherever the white man demands the separation, yet both his children and the white man's are being consigned to illiteracy wherever they are too few and poor to form separate schools.   In some mountainous parts of Kentucky there is but one colored school district in a *county*.   In railway travel the colored people's rights are tossed from pillar to post with an ever-varying and therefore more utterly indefensible and intolerable capriciousness.   In Virginia they may ride exactly as white people do and in the same cars.   In a neighboring State, a white man

may ride in the " ladies' car," while a colored
man of exactly the same dress and manners—
nay, his wife or daughter—must ride in the notor-
ious " Jim Crow car," unprotected from smokers
and dram-drinkers and lovers of vile language.
" In South Carolina," says the Charleston " News
and Courier," on the other hand, " respectable
colored persons who buy first-class tickets on any
railroad ride in the first-class cars as a right, and
their presence excites no comment on the part of
their white fellow-passengers.   It is a great deal
pleasanter to travel with respectable and well-
behaved colored people than with unmannerly
and ruffianly white men."   In Alabama the majority of the people have not made this discovery,
at least if we are to believe their newspapers.   In
Tennessee the law *requires* the separation of all
first-class passengers by race with equal accommodations for both ; thus waiving the old plea
of decency's exigencies and forcing upon American citizens adjudged to be first-class passengers
an alienism that has thrown away its last shadow
of an excuse.   But this is only the law, and the
history of the very case alluded to by our traditionist friends, in which a colored woman gained
damages for being compelled to accept inferior
accommodation or none for a first-class ticket, is
the history of an outrage so glaring that only a
person blinded to the simplest rights of human
beings could cite it in such a defense.

A certain daily railway train was supplied, according to the law, with a smoking-car, and two
first-class cars, one for colored and one for
whites. The two first-class cars were so nearly
of a kind that they were exchangeable. They
generally kept their relative positions on the
track ; but the " ladies' car " of the morning trip
became the " colored car " of the return, afternoon, trip, and *vice versâ*. But the rules of the
colored car were little regarded. Men, white and
black, were sometimes forbidden, sometimes allowed, to smoke and drink there. Says the
court, " The evidence is abundant to show that
the rule excluding smoking from that car was
but a nominal one, that it was often disregarded,
that white passengers understood it to be a nominal
rule, and that adequate means were not adopted
to secure the same first-class and orderly passage
to the colored passengers occupying that car as
was accorded to the passengers in the rear car.
Nor was the separation of the classes of the passengers complete. There is no evidence tending
to show that the white passengers were excluded
from the car assigned to colored passengers, and
it appears that whenever the train was unusually
crowded it was expected that the excess of white
passengers would ride, as they then did ride, in the
forward one of the two first-class cars. So, too,
it appeared that persons of color, of whom the
plaintiff was one, had several times occupied seats

in the rear car." A certain " person of lady-like appearance and deportment," one day in September, 1883, got aboard this train with a first-class ticket. She knew the train, and that, as the court states it, " in the rear car . . . quiet and good order were to so great an extent the rule that it was rarely if ever that any passenger gave annoyance by his conduct to his fellow-passengers." In the colored car there was at least one colored man smoking, and one white man whom she saw to be drunk. She entered the rear car and sat down, no one objecting. She was the only colored person there. The conductor, collecting his tickets, came to her. He was not disconcerted. Not long previously he had forbidden another colored person to ride in that car, who must also have been " of lady-like appearance and deportment," for when he saw this one he " supposed her to be the same person . . . intentionally violating the defendant's (Railroad's) rules and *seeking to annoy his other passengers*." Twice they exchanged polite request and refusal to leave the car ; and then, in full presence of all those " other passengers " whom this person of lady-like appearance and deportment was erroneously suspected of seeking to annoy," there occured a thing that ought to make the nation blush. The conductor laid hands upon this defenseless woman, whose infraction of a rule was interfering neither with the

running of the road, the collection of fares, nor
the comfort of passengers, and "by force removed her from her seat and carried her out of
the car. When near the door of the car the
plaintiff promised that she would then, if permitted, leave the car rather than be forcibly
ejected; but the conductor, as he says, told her
that her consent came too late, and continued to
remove her forcibly. On reaching the platform
of the car, plaintiff left the train." Judgment
was given for the plaintiff. But the point was
carefully made that she would have been without
any grievance if the "colored car" had only
been kept first-class. In other words, for not
providing separate first-class accommodations,
five hundred dollars damages; for laying violent
hands upon a peaceable, lady-like, and unprotected woman, nothing; and nothing for requiring such a one publicly to sit apart from passengers of the same grade under a purely
ignominious distinction. What! not ignominious?
Fancy the passenger a white lady, choosing, for
reasons of her own, to sit in a first-class "colored
car"; infringing, if you please, some rule; but
paying her way, and causing no one any incon-
venience, unsafety, or delay. Imagine her, on
insisting upon her wish to stay, drawn from her
seat by force, and lifted and carried out by a
black conductor, telling her as he goes that her
offer to walk out comes too late. If this is not

ignominy, what is it? To the commission and palliation of such unmanly deeds are we driven by our attempts to hold under our own arbitrary dictation others' rights that we have no moral right to touch, rights that in ourselves we count more sacred than property and dearer than life.

But we must not tarry. If we turn to the matter of roadside refreshment what do we see? Scarcely a dozen railroad refreshment-rooms from the Rio Grande to the Potomac,—is there one?—where the weary and hungry colored passenger, be he ever so perfect in dress and behavior, can snatch a hasty meal in the presence of white guests of any class whatever, though in any or every one of them he or she can get the same food, and eat with the same knife, fork, and plate that are furnished to white strangers, if only he or she will take a menial's attitude and accept them in the kitchen. Tennessee has formally "abrogated the rule of the common law" in order to make final end of "any right in favor of any such person so refused admission" to the enjoyment of an obvious civil right which no public host need ever permit any guest to mistake for a social liberty. As to places of public amusement, the gentlemen who say that "each [race] gets the same accommodation for the same money," simply—forget. The statement comes from Atlanta. But, in fact, in Atlanta, in Georgia, in the whole South, there is scarcely a place of public amusement—except the cheap museums, where there are no seated audiences—in which a colored man or woman, however unobjectionable personally, can buy, at any price, any but a second—sometimes any but a third or fourth-class accommodation. During a day's stay in Atlanta lately, the present writer saw many things greatly to admire ; many inspiring signs of thrift, stability, virtue, and culture. Indeed, where can he say that he has not seen them, in ten Southern States lately visited ? And it is in contemplation of these evidences of greatness, prosperity, safety, and the desire to be just, that he feels constrained to ask whether it must be that in the principal depot of such a city the hopeless excommunication of every person of African tincture from the civil rewards of gentility must be advertised by three signs at the entrances of three separate rooms, one for " Ladies," one for " Gentlemen," and the third a " Colored waiting-room " ? Visiting the principal library of the city, he was eagerly assured, in response to inquiry, that no person of color would be allowed to draw out books ; and when a colored female, not particularly tidy in dress, came forward to return a book and draw another, it was quickly explained that she was merely a servant and messenger for some white person. Are these things necessary to—are they consistent with—an exalted civiliza-

tion founded on equal rights and the elevation of the masses?

And the freedman's rights in the courts. It is regarding this part of our subject that our friends on the other side make a mistake too common everywhere and very common among us of the South. That is, they assume the state of affairs in more distant localities to be the same as that immediately around them. A statement concerning certain matters in Florida or Maryland is indignantly denied in Tennessee or Texas because it is not true of those regions; and so throughout. It is in this spirit that one of these gentlemen explains that in Georgia negroes are not excluded from the jury lists except for actual incompetency, and thereupon "*assumes* that Georgia does not materially differ from the other States." But really, in Tennessee they may not sit in the jury-box at all, except that in a few counties they may sit in judgment on the case of a colored person. While in Texas, at the very time of the gentleman's writing, the suggestion of one of her distinguished citizens to accord the right of jury duty to the colored people, was being flouted by the press as an "innovation upon established usage," and a "sentimental and utterly impracticable idea." This in the face of a State constitution and laws that give no warrant for the race distinction. So much for assumption.

The same mistake is repeated by the same writer in discussing the question of the freedmen's criminal sentences. No fact or person is brought forward to prove or disprove anything except for Georgia. And even the prosecuting attorney for the Atlanta circuit, brought in to testify, says, for the State's cities and towns, that the negro gets there " equal and exact justice before the courts "; but he is not willing to deny " a lingering prejudice and occasional injustice " in remote counties. Why, with nearly 6,000,000 freed people getting " full and exact justice in the courts whether the jury is white or black," why could there not be found *among them* two or three trustworthy witnesses to testify to this fact? Their testimony would have been important, for these lines are written within hand's reach of many letters from colored men denying that such is the case.

The present writer does not charge, and never did, that our Southern white people consciously and maliciously rendered oppressive verdicts against the freedman. On the contrary, it is plainly stated by him that they acted " not so maliciously as unreflectingly," and " ignorant of the awful condition of the penitentiaries." His only printed utterance on the subject is on record in " The Freedman's Case in Equity," and is too long to quote ; but he cited the *official reports* of our Southern State prisons themselves, and asked

how with their facts before us we are to escape
the conviction that the popular mind had been
seduced—as every student of American prison
statistics knows it has—by the glittering temptations of our Southern convict-lease system ; and
not one word of reply have we had, except the
assertion, which nobody would think of denying,
that the black man, often in Georgia, and sometimes elsewhere, gets an even-handed and noble
justice from white juries.

Have our opponents observed the workings of
this convict-lease system ? To put such a system
as a rod of punishment into the hands of a
powerful race sitting in judgment upon the misdemeanors of a feebler and despised caste would
warp the verdicts of the most righteous people
under the sun. Examine our Southern penitentiary reports. What shall we say to such sentences inflicted for larceny alone, as twelve,
fourteen, fifteen, twenty, and in one case forty
years of a penal service whose brutal tasks and
whippings kill in an average of five years ?
Larceny is the peculiar crime of the poorest
classes everywhere. In all penitentiaries out of
the South the convicts for this offense always
exceed and generally double the number of convicts for burglary. Larceny has long been called
the favorite crime of the negro criminal. What,
then, shall we say to the facts, deduced from
official records, that in the Georgia penitentiary

and convict camps there were in 1882 twice as
many colored convicts for burglary as for larceny, and that they were, moreover, serving
sentences averaging nearly twice the average of
the white convicts in the same places for the
same crime? This, too, notwithstanding a very
large number of short sentences to colored men,
and a difference between their longest and shortest terms twice as great as in the case of the
whites. For larceny the difference is five times
as great.[1] Shall we from these facts draw hasty
conclusions? We draw none. If any one can
explain them away, in the name of humanity let
us rejoice to see him do so. We are far from
charging any one with deliberately prostituting
justice. We are far from overlooking " the
depravity of the negro." But those who rest on
this cheap explanation are bound to tell us which
shows the greater maliciousness; for one man to
be guilty of hog-stealing or for twelve jurors to
send him to the coal mines for twenty years for
doing it? In Georgia outside her prisons there are
eight whites to every seven blacks. Inside, there
are eight whites to every eighty blacks. The
depravity of the negro may explain away much,
but we cannot know how much while there also
remain in force the seductions of our atrocious
convict-lease system, and our attitude of domi-

[1] Without counting the exceptional forty years' sentence mentioned.

nation over the blacks, so subtly dangerous to our
own integrity. Here is a rough, easy test that
may go for what it is worth : These crimes of
larceny and burglary are just the sort—since they
are neither the most trivial nor the most horrible
—to incur excessive verdicts and sentences, if
the prejudices of one class against another come
into the account. Now, what is the fact in the
prisons we have mentioned ? Of all the inmates
under sentence for these crimes nineteen-twen-
tieths are classed as of that race which we
" dominate" both out of and in the jury-box.
We ask no opinion on these points from the
stupid or vicious of either whites or blacks ; but
is it wise for us not to consider what may be
their effect upon the minds of the property-hold-
ing, intelligent, and virtuous portion of the " dominated " race ? Is it right?

IX. POLITICAL " SOLIDITY "—WHY AND TILL
WHEN?

In the same number of THE CENTURY that
contains " In Plain Black and White," appears an
open letter on " The Solid South." It tells us
that political " solidity," founded on the merits
neither of candidates nor questions, is an emphatic national and still greater local evil ; but
that the whites of the South " had to be solid,"
because they feared, and that they still fear, the

supremacy of the blacks. That if this fear were removed the whites would divide. Hence, we must first procure the division of the blacks; this is what it calls "the prerequisite." Is it? Is that a wise or just arbitration? Must the side that is immeasurably the weaker begin the disarmament? Is "*noblesse oblige*" untranslatable into "American"? We are only told that "once divide the negro vote and the 'solid South' is broken." True statement, but sadly antique. An old catchword pulled out of the rubbish of the Reconstruction strife. And why was the negro vote solid? The carpet-bagger and scalawag? It was so believed, and these—the most of them richly deserving their fate—were suppressed. What then? Less political activity among the blacks. But division? No. Then why were the blacks still "solid"? The open letter gives two causes: first, gratitude to the Republican party; second, fear of the Democratic. But these sentiments, it says, are fading out. Will their disappearance reveal the solid blacks divided? That depends on the matter that forms—what the open letter does not touch —the solid bottom of this question. But the more ambitious article in the same number of the magazine boldly confesses it when it decrees *the subserviency of the freedman's civil rights to the white man's domination.* As long as that continues to be or to threaten, the blacks will be solid. We—any people—would be so—would have to be so, in their place. Such a decree is equivalent to saying they must and shall be solid. Only let it be withdrawn and the solidity will vanish from the white vote and the black at the same instant.

This is what is coming. There is to-day no political party in America that is "solid" for this un-American and tyrannical principle; and the reason why the negro vote is a divided vote in the North to-day, and in the South shows more signs of dividing than ever before, is that the Republican party has grown fat and lazy concerning civil rights, while *Democratic* legislatures and governors, north, east, west, have been passing and signing civil rights bills, rooting out of the laws and of popular sentiment this heresy of domination by fixed class and race, and throwing to the winds "legal discriminations on account of color [which] are not based on character or conduct and have no relation to moral worth and fitness for civic usefulness, but are rather relics of prejudice which had its origin in slavery. I recommend," says the present Democratic governor of Ohio, from whose message we are quoting, "I recommend their total repeal." It is but little over a year since the Democrats joined the Republicans in the legislature of Connecticut in making liable to fine and imprisonment "every person who subjects or causes to be subjected any other person to the deprivation of any rights, privileges, or immunities secured or protected by the Constitution of the State or of the United States, on account of such person being an alien or by reason of his color or race." The time is still shorter since a Democratic majority in the legislature of New Jersey passed a bill of civil rights, as its own text says, "applicable alike to citizens of every race and color." Nor are they afraid of the names of things. "By direction of Governor Abbett," writes the executive clerk, "I send you copy of the *Civil Rights bill*[1] as passed by the Legislature and approved by him." In Indiana, while these pages were being written, Democrats were endeavoring to pass a civil rights bill. In May of last year the legislature at Albany passed a bill removing the last remaining civil disabilities from the colored people in the city of New York, by a *unanimous vote*, "three-fifths being present"; and the governor who signed the act is now President of the United States.

"Ah!" some will say, "these Northern Democrats do this in their ignorance; they do not know the negro." Is this the whole truth? Do not we forget that they have only gradually put aside from their own minds the very worst opinion of the negro that ever we had? To get where they are they have left behind the very same prejudices and misconceptions of citizens'

[1] Italicized only here.

rights that we are called to lay aside, and no others. Nay, even we assert facts now, that twenty years ago we used to say no man who knew the negro could honestly believe.

" But "—the answer comes again—" if they had the negro among them numerically power- ful, they would not venture to concede "—etc. Let us see : From Georgia, where, we are told, the freedman shall never enjoy " the policy indi- cated in the Civil Rights bill," pass across its eastern boundary, and lo, we are in a State under Southern Democratic rule, where the blacks are in the majority, yet which is not afraid to leave on the printed page, from the days of Recon- struction, a civil rights bill, not nearly so com- prehensive, it is true, but " fully as stringent," says its leading daily journal, " as any that Con- gress ever placed upon the statute-books," and attending whose enforcement " there is no friction or unpleasantness." This, in South Carolina !

May the time be not long delayed when her strong, proud people, that are sometimes wrong but ever conscientious and ever brave, not con- tent with merely not undoing, shall broaden the applications of that law until it perfectly protects white man and black man alike in the enjoyment of every civil right, and their hearts behind the law open to the freedman equally with the white man, as far as in him lies to achieve it, every civil reward of intelligence, wealth, and virtue. Then shall it still be as true as it is to-day that " No special harm has come of it." Not only so ; but the freedman, free indeed, shall along with his other fetters cast off the preoccupation in this question of civil rights which now engrosses his best intelligence, and shall become a factor in the material and moral progress of the whole land. Be the fault now where it may, he will not then outnumber the white man on the prison rolls eleven to one. And what is true of one Southern State is true of all. The temptations to which the negro—shut out from aspirations—now yields, will lose their power, and his steps be turned with a new hope and desire toward the prizes of industry, frugality, and a higher cultivation. Multiplying and refining his tastes, the rank energies of his present nature will not, as now, run entirely to that animal fecundity characteristic of all thriftless, reckless, unaspiring populations; his increase in civic value will be quickened, his increase in numbers retarded to a rate more like our own. And neither all the crops our sun-loved South can yield, nor all the metals and minerals that are under the soil made sacred by the blood of her patriots, can bring us such wealth and prosperity as will this change in the hopes and ambitions of our once unaspiring, time-serving slaves. The solid black will be solid no longer; but he will still be black.

X. THE GEOGRAPHY OF AMALGAMATION.

Is it not wonderful? A hundred years we have been fearing to do entirely right lest something wrong should come of it; fearing to give the black man an equal chance with us in the race of life lest we might have to grapple with the vast, vague afrite of Amalgamation; and in all this hundred years, with the enemies of slavery getting from us such names as negrophiles, negro-worshipers, and miscegenationists; and while we were claiming to hold ourselves rigidly separate from the lower race in obedience to a natal instinct which excommunicated them both socially and civilly; just in proportion to the rigor, the fierceness, and the injustice with which this excommunication from the common rights of man has fallen upon the darker race, has amalgamation taken place. Look—we say again—at the West Indies. Then turn and look at those regions of our common country that we have been used to call the nests of fanaticism; Philadelphia, Boston, Plymouth Church, and the like. Look at Oberlin, Ohio. For years this place was the grand central depot, as one might say, of the "Underground Railway"; receiving and passing on toward Canada and freedom thousands of fugitive slaves; weeping over them, praying over them, feeding them, housing them, hiding them in her bosom, defying the law for them, educating them, calling them sir and madam, braving no end of public contumely, and showing them every exasperating consideration. Look at Berea, Kentucky, where every kind thing contrivable that, according to our old ideas, could destroy a white man's self-respect and " spoil a nigger " has been practiced. What is the final fact ? Amalgamation ? Miscegenation ? Not at all. The letters of the presidents of these two famous institutions lie before the present writer, stating that from neither of them throughout their history has there resulted a single union of a white with a black person either within their precincts or elsewhere within the nation's wide boundaries. And of the two towns in which they are situated, in only one have there been from first to last three or four such unions. How have they been kept apart ? By law ? By fierce conventionality ? By instinct ? No ! It was because they *did not* follow instinct, but the better dictates of reason and the ordinary natural preferences of like for like. But, it is sometimes asked, admitting this much, will not undivided civil relations tend eventually—say after a few centuries—to amalgamation ? Idle question ! Will it help the matter to withhold men's manifest rights ? What can we do better for the remotest future than to be just in the present and leave the rest to the Divine Rewarder of nations that walk uprightly ?

XI. THE NATURAL-GROWTH POLICY.

There is a school of thought in the South that stands midway between the traditionists and us. Its disciples have reasoned away the old traditions and are now hampered only by vague ideas of inexpediency. They pray everybody not to hurry. They have a most enormous capacity for pausing and considering. " It is a matter," says one of them in a late periodical, " of centuries rather than decades, of evolution rather than revolution." The heartlessness of such speeches they are totally unconscious of. Their prayer is not so much that our steps may be logical as geological. They propose to wait the slow growth of civilization as if it were the growth of rocks, or as if this were the twelfth or thirteenth century. They contemplate progress as if it were a planetary movement to be looked at through the telescope. Why, we are the motive power of progress! Its speed depends on our courage, integrity, and activity. It is an insult to a forbearing God and the civilized world for us to sit in full view of moral and civil wrongs manifestly bad and curable, saying we must expect this or that, and that, geologically considered, we are getting along quite rapidly. Such talk never won a battle or a race, and the hundred years past is long enough for us of the South to have been content with a speed that the rest

of the civilized world has left behind. The tor-
toise won in the race with the hare, the race
didn't win itself. We have listened far too much
already to those who teach the safety of being
slow. "*Make haste* slowly," is the true emphasis. Cannot these lovers of maxims appreciate
that "Delays are dangerous"? For we have a
case before us wherein there is all danger and no
safety in floating with the tide.

Our fathers had such a case when African
slavery was first fastening its roots about the
foundations of our order of society. They were
warned by their own statesmen to make haste
and get rid of it. "You must approach the subject," cried the great Jefferson. "You must
adopt some plan of emancipation or worse will
follow"; and all the way down to Henry Clay
that warning was with more or less definiteness
repeated. But our fathers were bitten with the
delusion of postponement, and the practice of
slavery became an Institution. It grew, until
every element of force in our civilization—the
political arena, the sacred desk, the legislative
hall, the academical chair—all—were wrapped in
its dark shadow. Where might not our beloved
South be to-day, far on in front, but for that sad
mistake? At length, suddenly, rudely, slavery
was brought to an end. What that cost we all
know; yet let us hope there are many of us who
can say with our sainted Lee, not merely " I am

rejoiced that slavery is abolished "; but " I would cheerfully have lost all I have lost by the war, and have suffered all I have suffered, to have this object attained." [1]

Such was our fathers' problem. The problem before us is the green, rank stump of that felled Institution. Slavery in particular—the slavery of the individual man to his one master, which rested upon the law, is by the law abolished. Slavery in general—the subordination of a fixed ruled to a fixed ruling class—the slavery of *civil caste*, which can only in part, and largely cannot, be legislated away, remains. Sad will it be for our children if we leave it for their inheritance.

A Southern man traveling in the North and a Northern man just returned from a commercial tour of the South lately fell into conversation on a railway train. Said the Northerner, " What the South needs is to import capital, induce immigration, develop her enormous latent wealth, and let politics alone." " Sir," said the Southerner, " I know you by that sign for a commercial man, as I might know a hard student by his glasses and peering eyes. With you all things else are subsidiary to commerce ; hence, even commercially, you are near-sighted. It is true the South should seek those things you mention. They are for her better safety, comfort, and happiness. But

[1] See open letter in THE CENTURY for May, 1885.

what are politics ? In this land, at least, simply
questions concerning the maintenance or increase
of our safety, comfort, and happiness ; questions
that cannot be let alone, but must be attended to
as long as those things demand to be maintained
or increased."—The train stopped in a depot.
Men could be heard under the wheels, tapping
them with their hammers to test their soundness.
—" To ask us to let politics alone is to ask us to
leave the wheels of our train untested, its engine
unoiled, its hot boxes glowing, while we scurry
on after more passengers and passengers' fares ;
—which is just the way not to get them. Do
not ask it of us. Our scantiness of capital, mea-
gerness of population, and the undeveloped condition of our natural resources are largely owing,
this day, to our blindly insisting that certain
matters in our politics shall be let alone. It was
our letting them alone that brought Federal interference, and that interference has been withdrawn upon our pledge not to let them alone but
to settle them."

About a year ago the present writer visited the
thriving town of Birmingham, Alabama. Its
smelting furnaces were viewed with special interest. It was fine to see the crude ore of the earth,
so long trampled under foot, now being turned
by great burnings and meltings into one of the
prime factors of the world's wealth. But
another thought came with this, at sight of the

dark, brawny men standing or moving here and there with the wild glare of molten cinder and liquid metal falling upon their black faces and reeking forms. These were no longer simple husbandmen, companions of unfretted nature. If the subterranean wealth of the South is to be brought to the surface and to market all over the land, as now it is in this miniature of the great English Birmingham; if, as seems inevitable, the black man is to furnish the manual labor for this vast result, then how urgent is our necessity for removing from him all sense of grievance that we rightly may remove, and all impediment to his every proper aspiration, ere the bright, amiable influences of green fields and unsoiled streams, of leafy woods, clear sky, fragrant airs, and song of birds pass out of his life, and the sooty, hardening, dulling toils of the coal-pit and the furnace, and the huddled life that goes with it, breed a new bad knowledge of the power of numbers and a thirst for ferocious excitements, and make him the dangerous and intractable animal that now he is not. For our own interests, one and all of them, we ought to lose no time.

Our task is one whose difficulties can never be less, its facilities never be greater. We have no wars to distract and preoccupy. Here is a kindly race of poor men unlearned in the evil charms of unions, leagues, secret orders, strikes and bread-riots : looking not upon the capitalist as a natural

enemy; stranger to all those hostilities against
the richer and stronger world around them which
drive apart the moneyed man and the laborer
wherever living has become a hard struggle.
What an opportunity is ours to-day that will
never return when once it goes from us.   Look
at Ireland.

XII. "MOVE ON."

We occupy, moreover, a ground on which we
cannot remain.   It is not where we stood at the
war's end.   We approve the freedman's owner-
ship of himself.   We see and feel there is no
going back from universal suffrage.   And its
advocate may make a point of tremendous
strength in the fact that this very universality
of suffrage is what has bred in the South a new
sense of the necessity of public education for all
and of whatever else will enlighten and elevate
the lower mass.   Ignorance, penury, unintelligence, and the vices that go with them—the
bonds that hold the freedman down from beneath
—we are helping them to cast off.   But to cut
these loose and still lay on the downward pres-
sure of civil caste—is there any consistency in
this?   We cannot do it and respect our own
intelligence.   Socially we can do nothing for the
freedman or against him by rule or regulation.
That is a matter, as we might say, of specific
gravity.   But as to his civil rights, we cannot

stay where we are. Neither can we go backward.

To go forward we must cure one of our old-
time habits—the habit of letting error go uncon-
tradicted because it is ours. It grew out of our
having an institution to defend, that made a
united front our first necessity. We have none
now. Slavery is gone. State rights are safer than
ever before, because better defined; or, if unsafe,
only because *we* have grown loose on the subject.
We have nothing peculiar left save civil caste.
Let us, neighbor with neighbor, and friend with
friend, speak of it, think of it, write of it, get rid
of it. Ruskin's words seem almost meant for
our moment and region: " For now some ten or
twelve years," he says, " I have been asking every
good writer whom I know to write some part of
what was exactly true, in the greatest of the
sciences, that of Humanity." We speak for
this when we speak truly against civil caste. It
is caste that the immortal Heber calls " a system
which tends . . . to destroy the feelings of general benevolence." As far, then, as civil rights
are concerned, at least, let us be rid of it. This
done, the words North and South shall mean no
more than East or West, signifying only directions and regions, and not antipodal ideas of
right and government; and though each of us
shall love his own State with ardor, the finest
word to our ear as citizens shall be America.

To America we see irreversibly assigned the latest, greatest task in the "science of Humanity": to burst the last chrysalis of the national relation and consummate its last grand metamorphosis. Once it knew no wider bound than the tribal relation. But the day is on us at length, the problem is ours, and its great weight and responsibility and the honor of it when achieved rest and will rest on our Southern States. It is to make national harmony and unity broader than race ; to crystallize into fact the truth that national unity need not demand unification of race; to band together—without one single class disability or privilege diminishing or enhancing any individual's intrinsic value—in that one common, undistinguished enjoyment of every human civil right which only can insure national harmony and unity, two antipodal races ; two races that have no wish to, and for all we know never will, mingle their two bloods in one stream.

Nationalization *by* fusion of bloods is the maxim of barbarous times and peoples. Nationalization *without* racial confusion is ours to profess and to procure. It is not a task of our choosing. But our fathers, unawares, entailed it upon us, and we cannot but perform it. We cannot hold American principles in perfect faith and not do it. The good doctrine of liberty to all and license to none thrusts it inevitably into our hands. To make national unity without hybridity—the world has never seen it done as we have got to do it; but it is the business of every generation that comes into the world to bring into it better things than it has ever seen. We have got to build a nationality as free from all civil estrangement as from social confusion, yet wider than the greatest divergence of human races. This is the meaning of the great revolution upon us to-day. Daily the number increases of those who grasp it. A little while ago the whole nation rejected it. To reject it to-day is to be left behind the nation's best thought. How fast that thought is spreading in the South few know. Like the light of kindling watch-fires it is catching from mind to mind. The best men of the South are coming daily into convictions that condemn their own beliefs of yesterday as the antiquated artillery of an outgrown past; and to the present writer, as one who himself found this not easy, but hard, to do, it seems no improbability that our traditionist friends, even before this reply can reach them, may be found ranging themselves among that number, for the promotion of this revolution that everybody knows must come. To say what must, is to say what will be; and so shall the reproach of slavery, the greatest moral mistake made by the whole American nation, be swallowed up in the honor of this noble gain for the cause of humanity and universal peace.

THE CONVICT LEASE SYSTEM

THE CONVICT LEASE SYSTEM IN THE SOUTHERN STATES.[1]

I. A MODEL PRISON.

HERE and there in the United States a penal institution may be found that fairly earns the pride with which it is pointed out by the surrounding community. In the whole country there may be four or five such. The visitor to them admires the fitness of their architecture.

"Yes," the warden replies; "this is not a house of pleasure, and so we have not made it pretty. It is not an abode of crime, and so we have not made it ugly. It is not a place where men *seek* justice, and therefore we have not made it grandiose and majestic. But it is the house of chastisement,—of chastening punishment,—and so it is made solemn, severe, and calm."

The visitor praises the grave and silent decency of all the internal appointments.

[1] This essay was first printed in 1883; but although it was followed by many efforts for reform, they have failed because of the political power of the " penitentiary rings," and except a very inadequate, superficial improvement in Texas no changes of moment have taken place to put these pages materially out of date. (November, 1889.)

" Yes," responds the warden; " the peace and dignity of the State are here asserting themselves over the person of the prisoner who has violated them; there is no more room here for merriment or confusion than for strife."

The visitor extols the perfection of the sanitary arrangements.

" Yes," says the warden; " when the criminal was free and his life at his own disposal, he took no such care of it as this. He probably lived a sort of daily suicide. If he shortened his days, the State was, presumably, not to blame. But if we by malice or neglect shorten his days here, where he is our captive, we bring upon the State both blame and shame. For his life is in our custody, just as the clothing is with which he came here; the State, through ·its courts, has distinctly declined to tamper with it, and holds it subject to be returned to his own keeping, at the expiration of his confinement, in as good order as that in which it was received, the inevitable wear and tear of time alone excepted. Can the State maintain its peace and dignity as it should that commits breaches of trust inside its very prisons ? "

The visitor remarks that a wise benevolence is necessary even toward bad men.

" But," says the other, " it is not merely benevolence to bad men that puts in these elaborate sanitary appliances; it is the necessity of upholding the integrity and honor of the State."

The visitor shows his surprise at the absence
of all the traditional appliances for the correction
of the refractory. "Yet be certain," is the rejoinder, " a discipline, sure, prompt, and effectual
meets every infraction of rules. How else could
we have this perfection of order ? But it is a
discipline whose punishments are free from brutalizing tendencies, increasing dispassionately as
the culprit's passions increase, and relenting only
when he has repented." [1]

The visitor is impressed with the educative
value of the labor performed by the inmates.

" Yes," says the warden ; " send a man out
from here with knowledge of a trade, and may
be he will come back, but the chances are he
will not. Send him away without a trade, and
may be he will not come back, but the chances
are he will. So, for society's sake,—in the community's interest and for its safety,—these men
are taught certain trades that they cannot turn
to bad account. We do not teach burglars lock-
smithing."

Yet the visitor takes a momentary alarm.

[1] " Good order and discipline have been maintained during the
past year. There has not been one case of insubordination or
gross violation of any of the rules of the prison government;
not one case that required punishment, either for the purpose of
maintaining discipline or as penalty for an offense committed by
an individual prisoner."—" Annual Report of the Inspectors of
the State Penitentiary, Eastern District, Pennsylvania, 1882,"
p. 89.

"You put the housebreaker and the robber, the sneak-thief and the pickpocket into open competition with honest men in the community around them."

"Exactly," responds the other; "trying to live without competing in the fields of productive labor is just the essence of the crimes for which they were sent here. We make a short end of that."

The visitor looks with pleased interest at the statistical records of the clerk's office.

"We could not call our duty done without these," is the warden's response. "These are the keys to the study of the cause and prevention of crime. By these we weigh our own results. By these we uncover not only the convict and his crime, but society's and the State's own sins of omission and commission, whose fruits are these crimes and these criminals."

"After all," at length the visitor says, "tell me one thing more. Here where a prisoner is safe from fire and plague and oppression and temptation and evil companionship, and is taught thrift and skill, and has only to submit to justice and obey right rules, where is his punishment? How is this punishment at all?"

And the warden makes answer with question for question: "Had you a deformed foot, and an iron mold were made to close around it and press it into symmetrical shape and hold it so

would you ask where is the agony ? The punishment here is the punishment of a deformed
nature forced into superficial symmetry. It is
the punishment that captivity is to unrestraint;
that subordination and enforced self-control are
to ungoverned passion and inordinate vanity and
pride; that routine is to the love of idle adven-
ture ; that decorum is to the love of orgies ; that
temperance is to the love of drink; that loneli-
ness is to the social and domestic impulses; that
solitude and self-communion are to remorse. It
is all the losses and restraints of banishment,
without one of its liberties. Nothing tempers it
but the repentance and reform which it induces,
and these temper it just in degree as they are
genuine and thorough."

"And your actual results ? " asks the visitor.

" Of those who come here for their first offense,
a majority return to honest life."

" You have a model prison."

" No," says the warden, " not yet."

II. THE THEORY OF SELF-SUPPORT.

Now, the number of such prisons in America,
we say, may be counted on the fingers of one
hand. Communities rarely allow the prison its
rightful place among their investments of public
money for the improvement of public morals and
public safety. Its outlays are begrudged because

they do not yield cash incomes equal to their cash expenses. Legislatures, public schools, courts of justice, and departments of police are paid for by the people in the belief that they will and must be made to yield conditions and results necessary to be obtained, for whose absence no saving of public wealth can atone, and that ultimately, though indirectly, even on their pecuniary side, they are emphatically profitable. But when it is asked by what course of reasoning the prison is left out of this count, there is heard only, as one may say, a motion to adjourn. Society is not ready for the question.

The error is a sad one, and is deeply rooted. And yet it is a glaring one. A glance at the subject is enough to show that unless the money laid out in prisons is devoted to some end far better than the mere getting it back again, then legislatures, public schools, courts, and police all are shortened in their results, and a corresponding part of their expenses is rightly chargeable to the mismanaged prison. The prison is an inseparable part of the system; and the idea that the prison must first of all pay back dollar for dollar, if logically pushed on through the system, would close public schools, adjourn courts of justice, dissolve legislatures, and disband police. For not one of these could exist on a " self-supporting " basis.

Oftener, probably, than from any other one

source, this mistake springs from the indolent assumption that the call to make prisons what they ought to be is merely an appeal to public benevolence. It was so, in their earlier turn, with public hospitals and public schools ; and the effect was similar. For only here and there, if at all, did they find their best efficiency or a true public support, until society rose to the noble modesty that recognized them not as public charities, but as public interests. The management of a State's convicts is a public interest that still waits for the same sort of recognition and treatment. In many directions this has been partly conceded ; but there are few, if any, other State executives who would undertake to echo the lately uttered words of that one who said :

" In neither of the penitentiaries of this State has there ever been an attempt yet made to administer them on the vulgar, wicked, unworthy consideration of making them self-sustaining. In neither of them has it been forgotten that even the convict is a human being, and that his body and soul are not so the property of the State that both may be crushed out in the effort to reimburse the State the cost of his scanty food, and, at the end of his term, what then is left of him be dismissed, an enemy of human society."

The two dissimilar motives here implied govern the management of most American prisons. In a few the foremost effort is to make them yield, by a generous, judicious control, every result worth, to society's best interests, the money paid for it; that is, to treat them as a public interest. In a much larger number it is to seek such, and only such, good results as may be got without an appreciable excess of expense over income; that is, to treat them as appeals—and unworthy appeals—to the public charity. One motive demands first of all the largest results, the other the smallest net expense. They give rise to two systems of management, each of which, in practice, has its merits and drawbacks, and is more or less effectively carried out, according to the hands and minds under which it falls. These are known as the Public Accounts System and the Contract System.[1] Each has its advocates among students of prison science, and it is not the province of this paper further to press the contrast between them. It is truly the country's misfortune that in several States there is a third system in operation, a knowledge of whose real workings can fill the mind of any good citizen only with astonishment and indignant mortification.

By either of the two systems already named,

---

[1] The Contract System is often miscalled by the public press the Convict Lease System. But the Contract System merely, under careful restrictions, leases the convicts' labor within the prison walls during certain hours of the day and is entirely subordinated to the official management of the prison. While under the Convict Lease System the prison, the prisoner and the prison management are all farmed out into private control and an intelligent reformatory system is impossible.

the Public Accounts System and the Contract
System, the prison remains in charge of State
officials, the criminals are kept continually within
the prison walls, and the prison discipline rests
intact. All the appliances for labor—the workshops, tools, engines, and machinery—are provided by the State, and the convicts labor daily,
prosecuting various industries, in the Public Accounts System under their official overseers, and
in the Contract System under private contractors.
In degrees of more or less excellence, these industrial operations, whether under official directors or contractors, are carefully harmonized with
those features of the prison management that
look to the secure detention, the health, the discipline, and the moral reformation of the prisoner,
the execution of the law's sentence upon him in
its closest and furthest intent, and, if possible,
his return to the outer world, when he must be
returned, a more valuable and less dangerous
man, impressed with the justice of his punishment, and yet a warning to evil-doers. It is the
absence of several of these features, and sometimes of all, that makes the wide difference between these methods on the one hand and the
mode of prison management known as the Lease
System on the other.

III. EVIL PRINCIPLES OF THE LEASE SYSTEM.

Its features vary in different regions. In some, the State retains the penitentiary in charge of its officers, and leases out the convicts in gangs of scores or hundreds to persons who use them anywhere within the State boundaries in the execution of private enterprises or public or semi-public works. In a few cases the penitentiary itself, its appliances and its inmates, all and entire, are leased, sometimes annually or biennially, sometimes for five and sometimes for ten or even twenty years, and the convicts worked within or without the prison walls, and near to or distant from them, as various circumstances may regulate, being transferred from place to place in companies under military or semi-military guard, and quartered in camps or herded in stockades convenient to their fields of labor. In two or three States the Government's abandonment of its trust is still more nearly complete, the terms of the lease going so far as to assign to the lessees the entire custody and discipline of the convicts, and even their medical and surgical care. But a clause common to all these prison leases is that which allows a portion, at least, and sometimes all of the prisoners to be worked in parts of the State remote from the prison. The fitness of some lessees to hold such a trust may be estimated from the spirit of the following letters :

"OFFICE OF LESSEE ARKANSAS STATE PENITENTIARY,
"LITTLE ROCK, ARKANSAS, January 12, 1882.

"DEAR SIR : Your postal of request to hand; sorry to say cannot send you report, as there are none given. The business of the Arkansas State Penitentiary is of a private nature, and no report is made to the public. Any private information relative to the men will be furnished upon application for same.

"Very respectfully,
"ZEB. WARD, Lessee.
"Z. J."

"OFFICE OF LESSEE ARKANSAS STATE PENITENTIARY,
"LITTLE ROCK, ARKANSAS, July 2, 1882.

"DEAR SIR : Yours of —— date to hand and fully noted. Your inquiries, if answered, would require much time and labor. I am sole lessee, and work all the convicts, and of course the business of the prison is my private business. My book-keeper is kept quite busy with my business, and no time to make out all the queries you ask for. Similar information is given to the Legislature once in two years.

"Respectfully,
"ZEB. WARD."

The wonder is that such a scheme should not, upon its face, be instantly rejected by any but the most sordid and short-sighted minds. It is difficult to call its propositions less than an insult to the intelligence and humanity of any enlightened community. It was a Governor of Kentucky who, in 1873, justly said to his State Legislature: "I cannot but regard the present system under which the State penitentiary is leased and

managed as a reproach to the commonwealth.
. . . It is the system, not the officer acting under
it, with which I find fault."[1]

This system springs primarily from the idea
that the possession of a convict's person is an
opportunity for the State to make money; that
the amount to be made is whatever can be
wrung from him; that for the officers of the
State to waive this opportunity is to impose upon
the clemency of a tax-paying public; and that,
without regard to moral or mortal consequences,
the penitentiary whose annual report shows the
largest cash balance paid into the State's treasury
is the best penitentiary. The mitigations that
arise in its practice through the humane or
semi-humane sentiments of keepers and guards,
and through the meagerest of legislation, are
few, scanty, and rare; and in the main the notion
is clearly set forth and followed that a convict,
whether pilferer or murderer, man, woman, or
child, has almost no human right that the State
is bound to be at any expense to protect.

It hardly need be said that the system is not
in operation by reason of any malicious public
intention. On the part of lessees there is a most
unadmirable spirit of enterprise. On the part
of State officials there is a very natural eager-
ness to report themselves as putting money

[1] Quoted in " Transactions of the National Prison Congress,
St. Louis, 1874," p. 325.

into the treasury, and a low estimate of public sentiment and intelligence. In the people
at large there is little more than a listless oblivion, that may be reprehensible, but is not in-
tentional, unless they are to be judged by the acts
of their elected legislators, a rule by which few
communities would stand unaccused. At any
rate, to fall into the error is easy. Outlays for
the maintenance of police and courts are followed
with a jealous eye. Expense and danger keep
the public on the alert. Since neither police nor
courts can pay back in money, they must pay
back in protection and in justice. The accused
of crime must be arrested, the innocent acquitted
and exonerated, and the guilty sentenced to the
penalties of the laws they have violated. But just
here the careless mind slips into the mistake that
the end is reached; that to punish crime, no
matter how, is to deter crime; that when broken
laws are *avenged* that is the end; that it is enough
to have the culprit in limbo, if only he is made to
suffer and not to cost. Hence the public resolve,
expressed and enforced through legislators and
executive officers, to spend no more money on
the criminal than will promptly come back in
cash—nay, worse, to make him pay in advance;
and hence, too, a total disregard of all other results
for good or bad that may be issuing from the
prison walls. Thus it follows that that arm of
the public service by whose workings a large part

of all the immense labor and expenses of police and courts must become either profitable or unprofitable is handed over to the system which, whatever else of profound mischief its annual tables may betray or conceal, will show the smartest results on the cash-book. And thus we see, annually or biennially, the governors of some of our States congratulating their legislatures upon the fact that, by farming out into private hands whose single motive is money the most delicate and difficult task in the whole public service, that task is changed from an outlay that might have been made nobly advantageous into a shameful and disastrous source of revenue.

IV. IN TENNESSEE—THE SYSTEM AT ITS BEST.

If, now, we are to begin a scrutiny of this evil, we shall do well to regard it first as it presents itself in its least offensive aspect. To do this, we turn to the State prison, or prisons of Tennessee.

The State holds in confinement about one thousand three hundred convicts. The penitentiary is at Nashville, the capital. On the 5th of December, 1881, its workshops were accidentally destroyed by fire, and those which have taken their place are, if we may accept the warden's judgment, the finest south of the Ohio River.[1]

---

[1] Unfortunately for this pardonable boast, the boundary given cuts off all State prisons that exclude the lease management, except one small institution in West Virginia.

An advertisement from the Secretary of State, in a New Orleans paper of June 14, 1883, invites bids for a six years' lease of the " Penitentiary of Tennessee and the labor of the convicts, together with the building, quarry-grounds, fixtures, machinery, tools, engines, patterns, etc., belonging to the State." It is there asserted that the penitentiary has been conducted on this plan already for a number of years. The State's official prison inspectors remark, in their report of December 30, 1882 : "The Lease System, during our term of office, has worked harmoniously and without the least scandal or cause for interference on the part of the inspectors. Rentals have been promptly paid, and the prisoners worked in accordance with law and most humanely treated. . . To our minds there can be no valid objection raised to the Lease System, under proper restrictions, especially if as well conducted as for the past few years." They add the one reason for this conviction, but for which, certainly, there would be none : " A fixed revenue is assured to the State every year under the lease plan, as against an annual outlay under State management." The advertisement shows one feature in the system in Tennessee which marks it as superior to its application in most other States that practice it : the lessees employ such convicts as are retained " in the prison building at Nashville (many of whom are skilled laborers and of long-term sentence) in manufacturing wagons, iron hollow-ware, furniture, etc." The terms of the lease are required to be " not less than one hundred thousand dollars per annum, payable quarterly, clear of all expenses to the State on any account except the salaries of the superintendent, warden, assistant-warden, surgeon, and chaplain, which are to be paid by the State."

Here, then, is the Lease System at its best. Let us now glance in upon it for a moment through its own testimony, as found in the official report of its operations during the two years ending December 1, 1882. At the close of that term the State held in custody 1336 convicts. Of these, 685 were at work in the penitentiary, 28 were employed in a railway tunnel, 34 were at work on a farm, 89 on another farm, 30 in a coal-mine, 145 in another coal-mine, and 325 in still another. In short, nearly half the convicts are scattered about in " branch prisons," and the facts that can be gathered concerning them are only such as are given or implied in the most meager allusions. It appears that they are worked in gangs surrounded by armed guards, and the largest company, at least,—the three hundred and twenty-five,—quartered in a mere stockade. As the eye runs down the table of deaths, it finds opposite the names, among other mortal causes, the following: Found dead. Killed. Drowned. Not given. Blank. Blank.

Blank. Killed. Blank. Shot. Killed. Blank.
Blank. Killed. Killed. Blank. Blank. Blank.
Killed. Blank. Blank.[1] The warden of the penitentiary states that, " in sending convicts to the
branch prisons, especial care is taken to prevent
the sending of any but able-bodied men "; and
that " it has also been the custom to return the
invalid and afflicted convicts from the branch
prisons to this prison "—the penitentiary. Yet
the report shows heavy rates of mortality at these
branch prisons, resulting largely from such lingering complaints as dropsy, scrofula, etc., and
more numerously by consumption than by any
one thing else *except violence;* rates of mortality
startlingly large compared with the usual rates
of well-ordered prisons, and low only in comparison with those of other prisons worked under
the hands of lessees.

The annual reports (taken as they could be pro-
cured, one for 1880, three for 1881, and one for
1882) of five of the largest prisons in the United
States show that, from the aggregate population
of those prisons, numbering 5300 convicts, there
escaped during twelve months but one prisoner.
In all the State prisons of the country not kept

---

[1] One might hope these blanks were but omissions of ditto
marks, although such marks are not lacking where required in
other parts of the table; but the charitable assumption fails when
it would require us to supply them under " Sunstroke " and
opposite the date of December.

by the Lease System, with a population, at dates of reports, of 18,400, there escaped in one year only 63. But in the one year ending December 1, 1881, there escaped, from an average population of about 630 convicts at these Tennessee "branch prisons," 49 prisoners. Or, rather, there were 49 escapes; for some convicts escaped and were recaptured more than once or twice. The following year they numbered 50. If the tables in the report were correct,—it will be shown they are not,—we should know that the recaptures in the *two* years were about forty; but that which is not known is, what public and private expense in depredations on the one hand and the maintenance of police on the other, these ninety-nine escaped robbers, burglars, house-burners, horse-thieves, and swindlers, and these forty recaptures, have caused and are still causing. The superintendent of prisons, making exception, it is true, of one small establishment of less than a hundred population, whence over a third of these escapes were made, says the deputy wardens in charge "deserve credit for the manner in which they have carried out his instructions." Such is one feature of the Lease System under an exceptionally good administration of it. What a condition it had but lately come out of may be inferred from three lines found in the warden's report of the Texas penitentiary in 1880: "I noticed in a recent Tennessee report that, from an average force of less than 600 convicts, there were 257 escapes in two years."

The convict quarters in the main prison, at Nashville, are three separate stone wings, in each of which the cells rise one above another in four tiers. The total number of cells is 352. They are of three sizes. According to modern sanitary knowledge, a sleeping-room should never contain less than 800 cubic feet of air to each occupant; but, of these cells, 120 contain, each only 309 cubic feet of space; another 120 contain, each, but 175 feet; the remaining 112 contain but 162 feet each; and nearly every one of these cells has two inmates. Thus a majority of the inmates are allowed an air space at night less than the cubic contents of a good-sized grave. The physician of the penitentiary reports that the air breathed in these cells is "almost insupportable." He says of the entire establishment, "No amount of remodeling or tinkering can make it comfortable or healthy." The hospital he and others report as badly constructed and too small. "There is no place for dressing the dead except in the presence of all the sick in the hospital, or in the wing in the presence of more than two hundred convicts." Other details are too revolting for popular reading.

The female department of the prison "overlooks the prison yard in plain view and hearing of the male convicts." "No woman," says the warden, " should be sentenced to the Tennessee penitentiary until the State makes better provision for their care." " Had I the pardoning power, I would reprieve every woman now in the penitentiary and those who may be sentenced, until the State can or will provide a place to keep them, in keeping with the age in which we live." The chaplain reports these women as having "abandoned all hope and given up to utter despair, their conversation obscene and filthy, and their conduct controlled by their unrestrained passions." He indicates that he has abandoned all spiritual and moral effort among them ; but, it is to be regretted, does not state by what right he has done so.

The discipline of this main prison, as of the " branches," seems to be only such as provides for efficiency in labor and against insurrection and escape. The warden's report intimates that modes of punishment of refractory prisoners are left " to the discretion of wardens and inspectors." " When the labor is hired out," he says, " the lessee demands punishment that will not cause him to lose the labor of the man." Thus he lays his finger upon the fact that the very nature of the Lease System tends to banish all the most salutary forms of correction from the prison management. " Under the present·laws and custom," says this warden, " the Tennessee penitentiary is a school of crime instead of being a reformatory institution. . . . There are now about fifty boys in the penitentiary under eighteen years of age. . . . Nine-tenths of them leave prison much worse than when they came. . . . They are thrown into the midst of hundreds of the worst criminals the State affords, sleeping in the same cell with them at night, and working at the same bench or machine in the day. . . . The young and the old, the comparatively good and the vilest and most depraved, are thrown promiscuously together." [1]

Even that superficial discipline which obtains in the prison, addressed merely against physical insubordination, is loose, crude, and morally bad. The freedom of intercourse among the convicts is something preposterous. The State is actually put into the position of bringing together its murderers, thieves, house-breakers, highwaymen, and abandoned women, and making each acquainted with all the rest, to the number of about five hundred a year. In an intelligently conducted prison, each convict carries his food to his cell and eats it there alone ; but in this one the warden recommends that a dining-room be fitted up for 1200 persons. Convicts are given duties

[1] The roll of the Mississippi penitentiary shows, December, 1881, in a total number one-third less, seventy boys to have been received into the prison under eighteen years of age, some of them being but twelve and thirteen, sentenced for life and terms equivalent, in their probabilities, to a life sentence.

connected with the prison management; they are "door-keepers," and "wing-tenders," and "roll-callers." In one year the number of escapes from within its walls, not counting those made during the fire, was more than half as great as the total of escapes for an equal length of time from the State prisons of all New England, with New York, New Jersey, Pennsylvania, Maryland, Ohio, Indiana, and Illinois, where there were over 12,000 convicts. One *woman* escaped twice, and another one three times, both within the same ninety days.

The incapable simplicity of the prison's disciplinarians is pointedly shown again in a list of no less than 101 convicts recommended for executive clemency, some for having helped to put out the fire in December, 1881, some for holding mutineers in check on the same occasion, and some for running and telling on certain fellow-convicts who were preparing to escape in disguise. Reformatory discipline can hardly be imagined as reaching a lower degree of imbecility.

The chaplain's report is a bundle of crude generalities, marked by a serene ignorance of the badness of affairs, and by a total absence of any tabulated or other form of accurate or useful observation. Some spelling, some reading, regular Sabbath service, Sunday-school,—all is recounted in indefinite quantities, except the 33 admissions

into the "prison church." No feature is lacking
of that well-meant but melancholy farce which
religious prison work always must be when performed without regard to the unique conditions
of life to which it is addressed. During the win-
ter of 1881–'82, the chaplain preached sometimes
to the convicts at Ensley's farm, where "they
seemed to enjoy the services very much"; and
this is all he has to say of the place where men
were being "found dead," and "killed," and
"drowned," and "———"-ed. Nor was his silence
a mistaken discreetness; for he writes:

"The objects sought by imprisoning offenders being the security of society and the punishment and reformation of the guilty,
I am glad to say that these objects are certainly in a large measure being accomplished in many cases in the management of our
State Prison."

Having thus claimed a proprietary share in this
rotten institution, he wisely concludes with an
expression of timid uncertainty as to how many
of his "prison church" membership will finally
reach "the haven of eternal repose."

But are these bad conditions necessarily chargeable to the Lease System? No, and yes. They
have been dwelt upon to show with what a state
of affairs the system will content itself, its inspectors, the State legislators, and the community
at large. It has nothing in it to produce a
knowledge of and desire for a correct and honor-

able and truly profitable prison management. Its interests make directly against both individual and institutional reform. The plea of self-support on which it rests, the price it pays for its privileges, whether corruptly intended or not, are a bribe to officials and to public alike to close the ear against all suggestions of better things. For example, see the report of the two inspectors of the Tennessee prisons. Excepting a letter from another hand, quoted by them, their whole biennial report is less than one hundred lines. A little over half tells of the fire and the new workshops. A little less than half is given to the praise of the Lease System, upon the lonely merit of cash returns, and to a recommendation for its continuance. For the rest, they content themselves with pointing the Legislature to the reports of the superintendent, warden, physician, and chaplain of the penitentiary, whom, they say, "we indorse most heartily as attentive to their respective duties, and alive to every requirement of the law [which the warden reports as painfully barren of requirements] and the dictates of humanity in the discharge of their duty." However true this may be of the executive officers, it is certainly not true of the inspectors themselves. They do not certify to the correctness of a single roll or tabulated statement, or imply that they have examined any one of them. They do not present a statistical figure of their own, or recommend the taking of a single record among all the valuable registries that should be made, but are not, because the facts they would indicate are either absent or despised. Indeed, their silence is in a certain sense obligatory; for the omitted records, if taken, would condemn the system they praise, and the meager records that are given swarm with errors. It would have been hard for the inspectors to say anything worse for themselves than that they had examined the reports. The physician's is an almost unqualified denunciation of the whole establishment; the superintendent's is three-quarters of a page of generalities and official compliments; and the warden's tabulated statements confusedly contradict each other. Even the numerical counts are incorrect. One convict, distinctly named and described, appears in the list of escapes but once, and among the recaptured three times. One, reported escaped twice, is not once mentioned among the recaptures. Four convicts (one of them serving a nineteen years' sentence) reported among the recaptures are not on the prison roll, nor are they reported as pardoned, discharged, transferred, died, blanked, or in any other way disposed of. A convict, Zach. Boyd by name, under life sentence, expected soon to die of dropsy and recommended by the warden for executive clemency, is enrolled neither among the dead nor the living. The inference is irre-

sistible that the prison's officers do not know how
many convicts they have or should have.   In the
list of "Commutations," names occur repeatedly
that are not in any list of inmates on hand or removed or released.   Several convicts are reported
as white men when they escaped and as colored
when recaptured, and one or two pass through
two such transformations.   All search by the
present writer for occasion to lay these errors
upon the printer has proved unavailing.   The
fault is in the prisons themselves and the system
on which they are managed.   Such a condition
of accounts might be excused in the rosters of
a retreating army; but it is not to be believed,
while there is room for doubt, that the people of
an American State will knowingly accept such
stupid and wicked trifling with their State's good
name and the safety of society, or even such a
ghastly burlesque of net revenue.

V. IN NORTH CAROLINA.

Yet when we pass across the boundaries of
Tennessee and enter any adjoining State, excepting only Missouri, we find the same system in
operation, operating viciously, and often more
viciously than in Tennessee.   North Carolina,
during the two years ending October 31, 1880,
held in custody an average of 1090 convicts.
The penitentiary proper and its interior industries
were being controlled under public account.

Shoemaking, brickmaking, tailoring, blacksmith-
ing, etc., the officers report, were either already
profitable or could be made so, and their detailed
accounts of receipts and expenditures seem to
verify their assertions. The statistics of the
prison are given, not minutely or very compre-
hensively, but intelligently as far as they go, and
are valuable.

So much sunshine of right endeavor an unusually restrained Lease System lets in : the
Lease System itself exists only without the walls.
Only able-bodied convicts may be farmed out.
But just at this point the notion bred from a total
misconception of the true profits to be sought
—the notion that a penal establishment must
live upon its income—begins to show its fruit.
"Every enterprise that the board of directors,"
says its president, "have been able to devise for
using the labor that was compelled to remain in
the prison has been either summarily crushed in
its incipiency or seriously crippled in its progress
by the fact that we had not the means to carry
them to a successful issue. Attempted economy,
we believe, has proven a waste, and . . . the
State has suffered by a niggardly use of its resources. The [permanent] buildings, too, have
been carried too far to be now torn down, and
less costly ones erected in their stead. They
must, therefore, at some time, be completed ; and
so long as they are permitted to remain in their

present unfinished condition, they are subject to damage, from exposure to the weather, that will often necessitate work to be redone that would have been saved had they been steadily pressed to completion. There would, too, be incalculable economy in the police of the prison, if the convenient and compact building in progress of erection could speedily take the place of the scattered and imperfect wooden structures now in use ; and the suffering endured by the convicts in extreme cold weather, which is no part of their sentence, but has been unavoidable under the circumstances, would cease to be a source of anxiety to the board of directors and a reflection upon the power whose duty it is to relieve it."

The warden reports these temporary buildings as devoid of all means for warming them, badly ventilated, and entirely unfitted for use. A part, at least, of the inmates were, it seems, congregated in a stockade, which was " liable to tumble at any time." The prison physician pronounced these temporary quarters "the fruitful cause of many deaths." The population *within* this penitentiary was generally about three hundred. About eight hundred, therefore, were scattered about in companies under lessees, and in the two years 1879–80 were at different times at work on six different railways and one wagon road. What their experiences were at these places can be gathered, by one at a distance, only from one

or two incidental remarks dropped by the prison
officers in their reports and from the tabulated
records of the convict movement. There is no
hospital record given concerning them, nor any
physician's account of their sickness. When
they drop off they are simply scored as dead.
The warden says of them that many had "taken
their regular shifts for several years in the
Swannanoa and other tunnels on the Western
North Carolina Railroad, and were finally returned to the prison with shattered constitutions
and their physical strength entirely gone, so that,
with the most skillful medical treatment and the
best nursing, it was impossible for them to re-
cuperate."

But such remarks convey but a faint idea of
the dreadful lot of these unfortunate creatures.
The prison physician, apologizing for the high
death-rate within the walls, instances twenty-one
deaths of men " who had been returned from the
railroads completely broken down and hopelessly
diseased." And when *these deaths are left out* of
the count, the number of deaths *inside* the walls,
not attributable to *outside* hardships, amounted,
in 1880, to just the number of those in the
prisons of Auburn and Sing-Sing in a population
eight times as large. Ten-elevenths of the deaths
for 1879 and 1880 were from lingering diseases,
principally consumption. Yet, year in and year
out, the good citizens of Raleigh were visiting

the place weekly, teaching Sunday-school, preaching the gospel, and staring these facts in the face.

Now, what was the death-rate among the convicts working at railroad construction? The average number of prisoners so engaged in 1879 and 1880 was 776. The deaths, including the 21 sent back to die in prison, were 178, an annual death-rate of nearly eleven and a half per cent., and therefore greater than the year's death-rate in New Orleans in 1853, the year of the Great Epidemic. But the dark fact that eclipses everything else is that not a word is given to account for the deaths of 158 of these men, except that 11 were shot down in trying to escape from this heartless butchery.

In the light of these conditions, the warden's expressed pleasure in the gradual decrease in prison population since 1877 in North Carolina seems rather ill grounded and not likely to last. It is certainly amazing that men of the sincerest good intentions can live in full knowledge of such affairs, or, at least, within easy reach of the knowledge, and not put forth their protest against the system that fosters and perpetuates it. The North Carolina prison, it may be repeated, is managed, within its walls, on the public account; but it is the Public Accounts System suffocated under the Lease System and stabbed by the glittering policy of self-support. In 1880 alone the *Lease System, pure and simple,* set free upon the people of North Carolina, from its railroad gangs, 123 escaped criminals. The prison added 12 more. The recaptures numbered 42. Ninety-three remained at large; just 5 more than the *total* escapes for an equal period in every State prison of every State in this country, excepting the other eleven managed in whole or part upon the Lease System. The moral effect of such a prison life on men herded in stockades may be left to the imagination; but one other fact must be noted. In the two years 1879–80 there were turned into this penitentiary at Raleigh 234 youths under twenty years of age, not one of whom was under sentence for less than twelve months.

It only remains to be asked, For what enormous money consideration did the State set its seal upon this hideous mistake? The statement would be incredible were it attempted to give other than a literal quotation. "Therefore it will be seen," says the warden at the bottom of his résumé of accounts, "that the convicts have earned $678.78 more than the prison department has cost for the two years ending October 31, 1880."

VI. IN KENTUCKY.

In Kentucky the management of the State prison seems to be in a stage of transition. Facts that need no mention here[1] make allusion to it a particularly delicate task. Yet the writer may not assume that any one would desire that the truth be left unsaid. Upon the candor and generosity not only of Kentuckians, but of all the communities whose prisons come under this review, must the writer throw himself, trusting to find his words received in the same spirit of simple good citizenship in which they are offered.

After long experience with the Lease System, there was passed in May, 1880, an "Act to provide for the government, management, and discipline of the Kentucky penitentiary," by which the prison passed back from other hands into those of the State's appointed officers. The Lease System was not discarded; but certain very decided modifications were made in it, leaning toward the Contract System. The report made by the prison officers and board, eighteen months later, bears a general air of the sad confusion that commonly belongs to a late and partial extrication from disaster. It affords a retrospective view of the old system extremely

---

[1] At Louisville, Kentucky, where the convention before which this paper was read was then enjoying the hospitality of the State.

unflattering; but it also gives evidence that certain State officers, conspicuously the Governor,
were making an earnest and sagacious effort to
reform the entire penal system of their commonwealth. Yet it seems plain again that they are
not a little handicapped by that false popular idea
of the prison's place in the State's governmental
economy, upon which the Lease System thrives
while the convict falls into moral and physical
ruin and society's real interests are sold for old
rags. It may be assumed that there is a reserved
determination on the part of those who have
taken the matter in hand, to raise the work of
reform to the plane it should occupy as soon as
the general sentiment can be brought to require
it; but, meantime, the State's penal system has
risen, from something worse, only to the level cf
the system in North Carolina.

The officers whom the State, pursuant to its
scheme of renovation, placed in charge, put that
scheme into practice, to use their own words,
"whenever the costs of doing so involved only
a small outlay." The building that contains the
prisoners' cells, found "infested with all kinds of
vermin known to institutions of the kind," with
bad ventilation and rat-eaten floors was purged,
by convict labor, with coal-oil, fire, whitewash,
and tar. The grounds around the women's quarters, "low and marshy, covered with water, in
rainy weather, ankle-deep for days," were filled

up. " Long rows of shanties or sheds, . . . unsightly and inflammable in the extreme," long used in the hackling of hemp, were torn away. The hospital and chapel were cleaned and kept clean. Religious services were regularly afforded by an official chaplain and at intervals by a Catholic priest, and Sabbath instruction gradually took shape with (let it be said to their praise) members of the Governor's own family in charge. The diminutive and dilapidated library was put into shape and new books were added. But from here on, the friends of the prison could only pray for aid and relief. The principal industry continued to be, as it had been for many years, working in hemp, under circumstances that made it a distressing and unhealthful hardship. On the 1st of last January, 350 men were working in that department without ventilation or bath, and, says the warden, "the dust so dense that it is frequently impossible to recognize a man twenty feet distant."   " It is certainly an act only of common humanity that the evil created should be counteracted by good and ample bathing facilities."   In the hospital, as a fit adjunct to the hemp department, there were, in 1881, 144 cases of inflamed eyes and 202 of acute bronchitis. The kitchen was not adapted to the proper cooking of the prisoners' food, and the hospital's response was 616 cases of acute disease of the bowels and 101 of impoverishment of the blood.

There was an entire absence of an intelligent *trained* reformatory treatment, in accordance with a knowledge of criminal character, recognition of the criminal's unforfeited rights, and proper prison discipline. In this shape stood matters at the beginning of the year 1882, as viewed from without. The inside history can only be conjectured ; but we get one glimpse of the convict's sentiment toward his choking, blinding, life-shortening daily task in the fact that, within the eighteen months of the new régime, five men purposely mutilated their hands so as to compel the amputation of fingers, and two others cut off, each, a hand at the wrist. What the fortunes of the convicts leased out upon railroad construction were and are, we are given no clew by which to tell; the report contains no returns from them, and we have only the same general assurance that all is well that is given as to those in Tennessee and North Carolina.

VII. IN SOUTH CAROLINA.

Another view of the Lease System under limitations is afforded in the " Annual Report of the Board of Directors of the South Carolina Penitentiary for the fiscal year ending October 31, 1881." The prison is not only under a full corps of State officers, but, like the North Carolina prison, it is conducted on public account, the convicts only being leased,

and of these only such as are sent beyond the
prison's walls.   Yet the overwhelming consideration of self-support makes the spirit of the
Lease System dominant over all.   The reformatory features are crude, feeble, and purely accidental.   The records are meager.   The discipline
is of that poor sort which is vaguely reported as
"administered only when necessary," addressed
simply to the prisoner's safe custody and the
performance of his tasks.   The escapes, from an
average population of 632, were 36 ; the recaptures, 21.   Most likely, to the popular eye, the
numbers are not startling ; but, if we look
around to compare them with the record of some
properly ordered prison of the same population,
we see the warden of the Maryland penitentiary,
under contract management, admitting with full
explanation and apology the escape of one prisoner, the first in ten years.   The number of
escapes reported from the South Carolina prison
would have been forty, had not four escaped convicts been " found drowned " within two or three
days after their escape.   A report with which
such numbers will compare favorably can be
found only by turning to other leased prison
forces.   One reason why it may there be found
is that, in South Carolina, almost alone, a penalty
attaches to the lessees for each escape.   " There
is now due the State," says the report, "in penalties for the escape of convicts under contract

[meaning leased convicts] about $25,000." In
the chaplain's report, as in all chaplains' reports
under the Lease System, and probably in many
under better systems, is seen the familiar con-
junction of pious intention with a strange oversight of the inadaptability, to the incarcerated
criminal, of the ordinary technical methods of
religion in society. What response can there be
but a weary smile to the complacent announce-
ment that in this prison "there are now about
one hundred men and women who can repeat
the Ten Commandments, the Lord's Prayer, the
Apostles' Creed, and the whole of Capers' Cate-
chism." But the humor fades out when it is
added, "We have also a Sunday-school, regularly
conducted by *intelligent convicts*." " I regard the
State Penitentiary, as designed by its originators,
as a great reformatory school, and I am happy
to believe, from personal observation, . . . that
this prime leading object is . . . being faithfully
carried out." So writes this evidently sincere
and zealous divine, in the face of the fact that
the very foundation principles of reformatory
treatment were absent, and that constantly a
larger number of convicts were kept beyond his
reach than were left for him to preach to.

One of the peculiar temptations which the
Lease System holds out to the communities em-
ploying it, as such communities are represented
in the jury-box, needs a moment's careful notice.

The States where this system is in vogue are now, and have been for some years, enjoying a new and great development of their natural resources and of other industries than that colossal agricultural system that once monopolized their attention. There is, therefore, a vigorous demand for the opening and completion of extensive public works,—mines, railways, turnpikes, levees, and the like,—and for ways and means for getting them done as quickly and cheaply as possible. Now, it is with these potent conditions in force that the Lease System presents itself as the lowest bidder, and holds forth the seductive spectacle of these great works, which everybody wants and no one wants to pay for, growing apace by convict labor that seems to cost nothing. What is the consequence? We might almost assert beforehand that the popular sentiment and verdict would hustle the misbehaving, with shocking alacrity, into the State's prison under extravagant sentences or for trivial offenses, and sell their labor to the highest bidder who will use them in the construction of public works. The temptation gathers additional force through the popular ignorance of the condition and results of these penitentiaries, and the natural assumption that they are not so grossly mismanaged but that the convict will survive his sentence, and the fierce discipline of the convict camp "teach him to behave himself."

But there is no need to reason from cause to effect only. The testimony of the prisons themselves is before us, either to upset or else to establish these conjectures. A single glance at almost any of their reports startles the eye with the undue length of sentences and the infliction of penalties for mere misdemeanors that are proper only to crimes and felonies. In the Georgia penitentiary, in 1880, in a total of nearly 1200 convicts, only 22 prisoners were serving as low a term as one year, only 52 others as low a term as two years, only 76 others as low a term as three years; while those who were under sentences of ten years and *over* numbered 538, although ten years, as the rolls show, is the *utmost* length of time that a convict can be expected to remain alive in a Georgia penitentiary. Six men were under sentence for simple assault and battery,—mere fisticuffing,—one of two years, two of five years, one of six years, one of seven, and one of eight. For larceny, three men were serving under sentence of twenty years; five were sentenced each fifteen years; one, fourteen years; six, twelve years; thirty-five, ten years; and one hundred and seventy-two, from one year up to nine years. In other words, a large majority of all these had, for simple stealing, without breaking in or violence, been virtually condemned to be worked and misused to death. One man was under a twenty years' sentence for "hog-stealing." Twelve men were sentenced to the South Carolina penitentiary, in 1881, on no other finding but a misdemeanor commonly atoned for by a fine of a few dollars, and which thousands of the State's inhabitants are constantly committing with impunity—the carrying of concealed weapons. Fifteen others were sentenced for mere assault and assault and battery. It is to be inferred—for we are left to our inferences—that such sentences were very short; but it is inferable, too, that they worked the customary loss of citizenship for life. In Louisiana, a few days before the writing of this paper, a man was sentenced to the penitentiary for twelve months for stealing five dollars' worth of gunny-sacks.

VIII. IN GEORGIA.

The convict force of Georgia, already more than once alluded to, presents the Lease System under some other peculiarly vicious aspects. For example, the State is bound by, and is now in the fourth year of, a twenty years' lease. The convicts, on October 20, 1880, were 1185 or 1186 in number (the various exhibits of the biennial report differ widely in some of their statements). They were consigned to three penitentiaries in three different counties, each of which had "several branch camps." Thus they were scattered about in eleven camps over at least seven counties. The assurance of the "principal keeper" is that in all these camps they are humanely treated. Every "permanent camp" has a hospital, a physician, and a chaplain. But there are other camps that have none. Reports from other officials and from special committees of citizens repeat the principal keeper's assurance in the same general terms. And yet all these utterances unconsciously admit facts that betray the total unfitness of the management for the ends it ought to have in view and its gross inhumanity. From the "General Notice to Lessees" the following is taken, with no liberties except to italicize :

"In all cases of *severe illness* the *shackles* must be promptly removed." "The convicts shall be turned off of *the chain* on the Sabbath and allowed to recreate in and about the stockade." Elsewhere the principal keeper says, "When a convict is sick, the chains are to be taken off of him." As to the discipline, he reports 35 escapes (7 burglars, 3 house-burners, 9 murderers and would-be murderers, 1 forger, 3 robbers, 7 thieves, and others whose crimes are best unmentioned), with no recaptures ; and the surgeon reports nine men killed, three of them by fellow convicts. "You will observe the death-rate to have greatly decreased in the last two years," says the principal keeper ; but the death-rate, when observed, was found to have decreased only to about twice

the rate of properly planned and managed establishments of the kind.   This, he reports, is one-
half what it had been.   His tabulated statements
relating to the convicts, though lamentably scanty,
reveal an amount of confusion behind them that
is hard to credit.   One table, purporting to show
the whole 1186 convicts in confinement, classified
by the crimes under which they were sentenced,
has not a single correct number in it, and is an
entire hundred short in its true total.   The numbers, moreover, are so far out of the way that
they cannot possibly be the true exhibit of some
other date substituted in error.   They report 184
under sentence for burglary, whereas the roll
shows 467, and they entirely omit 25 serving
sentence for forgery, and 23 for robbery.

IX. THE PARDONING POWER.

We have already noticed, in the prison and
convict camps of this State, the feature of cruel
sentences.   Let us look at another; to wit, lavish
pardons.   It is but typical of the prisons under
the Lease System, wherever that is found in
unrestrained operation.   Here may be seen a
group of penal institutions, the worst in the
country by every evidence of their own setting
forth : cruel, brutalizing, deadly ; chaining, flogging, shooting, drowning, killing by exhaustion
and exposure, holding the criminal out to the
public gaze, publishing him to the world by

name and description in its reports when he goes in, every alternate year while he stays in, and when he dies or goes out; putting under foot every method of reform worthy of prison science, mocking such intelligent sense of justice and mercy as he may have, and doing everything that can be done to make his heart and conscience harder than the granite of his prison walls. Yet these prisons are sending forth from their gates a larger percentage of their populations, pardoned, than issues in like manner from all the prisons of the country managed on intelligent reformatory systems. Nor can the fault be confidently imputed, as is often hastily done, to political design or mere pliability in State governors. The horrors of the convict camps, best known to the executive, the absence of a discipline calculated to show who is worthy of clemency, the activity of outside friends usurping this delicate office, are potent causes; and the best extenuation that can be offered is that a large proportion of these pardons is granted not because the prisoner has become so good, but because the prison is so bad.

X. IN TEXAS.

This is conspicuously the case in Texas. In the two years ending October 31, 1880, the Governor pardoned one hundred State convicts from the Huntsville (Texas) penitentiary. Over one-fourth were *children from ten to sixteen years of age*, and nearly another fourth, says the superintendent, " were hopelessly diseased, blind, crippled, or demented, . . . simple objects of pity, the sight of whom would have excited commiseration in hearts of stone."

For some years past Texas has had in custody about two thousand convicts at once. They are under the Lease System, some of whose features, at least, give dissatisfaction to the State's prison directors and to its Legislature. The working of convicts remote from the prison, though practiced, is condemned, and the effort is being made to bring the management into conformity with a statute that requires as many of the convicts as can be to be employed within the penitentiary walls. Two different reports of the directors, covering a period of four years, impress their reader as the utterances of men of the best disposition, sincerely desiring to promote humanity and the public good, but handicapped, if not themselves in some degree misled, by the error of making self-support the foremost consideration in all their estimates of prison methods.

" To provide for their employment, so that they will cease to be a *burden upon the taxpayers of the country*," would be counted a strange proposition to apply to courts, schools, or police, yet is assumed by them, as a matter of course, to be applicable to prison populations, and so becomes the barrier from which they recoil, and which they have allowed to throw them back into the mire of the lease system. " This problem," they say, " has long engaged the attention of philanthropists and statesmen." But they mistake. The real problem that has engaged such is, How to procure the most honorable and valuable results, and to pay for them whatever is necessary and no more. It was, unfortunately, under the shadow of these mistakes that the Texas board went so far as to " consider very seriously as to whether it should not adopt the Public Accounts or the Contract System," only to reject the one and to fail to get bids on the other. As a result the State stands to-day bound, for fourteen years to come, by the Lease System, the worst prison system in Christendom, a system that cannot be reconciled with the public honor, dignity or welfare. The board intimates plainly that this Lease System is not its choice, or at least would not be but for the nightmare of self-support. As it is, they strive to make the best of a bad matter. How bad it has been and is, a few facts will show.[1]

It is said of the Huntsville penitentiary, Texas

[1] The Legislature has rejected and annulled this lease, but

(an additional one has just been built at Rusk), that it was built " on the old plan, looking altogether to security, and without any regard to proper ventilation or the health or comfort of the inmates, . . . the cell buildings . . . to a considerable extent cut off from light and air, and in constant danger of destruction from fire." The prison board erected a new cell building to take its place, in which each cell has a cubic content of 384 feet, and, says the board, " can comfortably accommodate two men." This gives each occupant an air space one-quarter of the minimum necessary to health. Yet this was a great improvement. It may be mentioned in passing, as an incident very common under the Lease System, that about the same time a lot of machinery, the property of the State, valued on the inventory of one lessee after another at $11,600, was sold for $681, and the proceeds laid out in fifty-one breech-loading, double-barreled shotguns. The following is from the superintendent's biennial report of October 31, 1880: " The most usual mode of punishment practiced at outside camps is by stocks. . . . Most of the sergeants, in order to make it effective, have lifted the convicts on the ball of the foot, or tiptoe, . . . jeopardizing not only health but life. The [present] lessees . . . abolished the use of stocks at

under a public accounts system has retained the most odious features of the Convict Lease System.

their wood camps, and I rejoice that you [the directors] have determined to abolish them alto-gether. On many of the farms sergeants have been in the habit of . . . whipping, as well as permitting their guards to do so, without first obtaining an order from the board of directors, as required by law." Of illegal punishments he says: "We have been compelled to discharge sergeants and a great number of guards on account of it. . . . I am satisfied that many escapes have been caused by illegal punishments and by cursing and threats." The spirit of this officer's report does him honor throughout.

One can turn again only to leased prisons else-where, to find numbers with which to compare the ghastly mortality of some of these Texas convict camps. Men in large numbers, "who have contracted in the miserable jails of the State incurable diseases, or whose systems have been impregnated with diseases from having led lives of debauchery and dissipation, are put to the hardest manual labor and . . . soon break down in health." "Sick convicts are crowded into the same building containing well convicts, and cannot have proper nursing and quiet, even if they have good medical attention." "Frequently sergeants, believing that convicts are trying to play off, have kept them at work when, in fact, they were seriously ill, . . . or have tried to physic them themselves." On railroad construction the average *annual* rate of mortality, for 1879 and 1880, was 47 to the thousand, three times the usual death-rate of properly managed American prisons ; at plantation labor it was 49 ; at the iron-works it was 54 ; and at the wood-cutting camps more than half the entire average population died within the two years.   So much as to the rate.   The total *number* of deaths in the period was 256, of which only 60 occurred in the prison hospital, the rest in the camps.   Nor was any considerable fraction of them by con-tagious diseases.   They were from congestions of the brain, the stomach, and the bowels ; from scurvy, dropsy, nervous fever, malaria, chronic diarrhœa, general debility, pneumonia.   Thirty-five died of gun-shot wounds, five of "*wounds miscellaneous.*"   Of three, the cause of death was " not stated."   Three were drowned, four were sunstruck, two committed suicide, and two were killed by the explosion of a boiler.   And all was reported without a word of apology or explanation.   The whole thirty-five who were shot to death were shot in attempting to escape " from forces at work outside the prison walls." " In nearly all these cases the verdict of a coro-ner's jury has stated that the guard acted in dis-charge of his duty."   As to the remainder, we know not what the verdicts were or whether there were any ; nor do we know how many vain attempts were made to escape ; but we know

that, over and above the deaths, there were
treated in the prison hospital—where so few of
the outside sick ever arrived—fifteen others with
gunshot wounds and fifty-two with " wounds miscellaneous."

We know, too, by the record, that four men
did escape from within the prison walls, and three
hundred and sixty-two from the gangs outside.
In the interest of the Texas taxpayer, from
whom the Lease System is supposed to lift an
intolerable burden, as well as for society at large,
it would be well to know what were the favorite
crimes of these three hundred and sixty-six
escaped felons (since unreformed criminals generally repeat the same crimes again and again),
what moral and material mischief one hundred
and twenty-three of them did before they were
recaptured, and what the record will be of the
two hundred and forty-three remaining at large
when the terms they should have served have
expired. These facts are not given; we get
only, as it were, a faint whiff of the mischief in
the item of $6900 expended in apprehending one
hundred of them.

And yet this is the operation of the Lease
System under a Governor who was giving the
State prison and its inmates a far more rational,
humane, and diligent attention than is generally
accorded them by State executives, albeit such
officers are not as negligent in this direction as

they are generally supposed to be ; under a warden, too, who, if we read rightly between the lines
of his report, is a faithful and wise overseer ; and
even under lessees whom this warden commends
as " kind and humane gentlemen." We have both
the warden's and the directors' word for it, that
this disciplinary and sanitary treatment of the
convicts was " a very decided improvement " on
what it had been. The question remains, What
may the system do where it is a State's misfortune to have a preoccupied Governor and unscru-
pulous prison lessees ? It is a positive comfort
to know that for two years more, at least, the
same officials and lessees remained in charge,
that a second prison was added to the old one
and a third projected, and that the total mortality
was reduced by the abolition of the wood-cutting
camps.

But it is far otherwise to know by the report
for 1881–82 that the death-rate is still enormous,
and has increased in the prison and in most of
the camps; that the number of men committed
to hospital with gunshot and " miscellaneous "
wounds was fifty-two ; that in the mortality lists
are three suicides, six sun-strokes, and thirty-six
victims of the breech-loading double-barreled
shot-guns; that there passed through hospital
fifty-one cases of scurvy ; and that there were
three hundred and ninety-seven escapes and but
seventy-four recaptures.

It may be enough attention has already been
given to chaplains' reports in these so-called penitentiaries, but the one for the Texas prison com-
pels at least a glance. It makes sixteen lines of
letter-press. White men's prayer-meeting on
Sunday at one hour, colored men's at another,
general Sunday-school at another, preaching at
another. These services are believed to have
been fruitful of good; it is hoped "that some
will leave the prison reformed men"; but there
is not the record of one positive result, or a single
observation registered looking to the discovery
of a result, either intellectual, moral, or religious,
concerning hundreds of men whose even partial
reformation would be worth to the State—if it
must be reduced to money value—tens of thousands of dollars. Two lines of the report are
certainly unique : " We endeavor to enlist all the
men in this service [the Sunday-school] we can,
and try to suppress all differences of opinion
which are calculated to engender strife."

A single ten thousand dollars is the State's
annual share in what are called the profits of this
system of convict control. Were the convicts
managed under the Public Accounts System at
an annual loss of a like amount (which need not
be), making a difference of twenty thousand dollars, and were the burden lifted from the mass of
the one million six hundred thousand inhabitants
of Texas and thrown entirely upon the shoulders

of one hundred thousand tax-payers, it would be just one dime a year to each shoulder. But it would save the depredations of nearly two hundred escaped convicts per year, whatever they might be; such reprisals as about four hundred others, annually liberated and turned loose upon society, may undertake as an offset for the foul treatment they have undergone in the name of justice, and the attendant increase in the expenses of police; and the expenses of new trials and convictions for the same old crimes committed over again by many who might have in whole or in some degree reformed, but instead were only made worse. And two things more it would save—the honor of the State and the integrity of the laws and of the courts. For one thing, however, the people of Texas are to be congratulated: that they have public servants ready—let the people but give the word—to abjure the Lease System with all its horrid shams and humiliating outrages, and establish in its place a system of management that shall be first honorable and morally profitable, and then as inexpensive as may be.

XI. IN ALABAMA.

Something like the same feeling was displayed
by the Governor and some others in the State of
Alabama in 1882.   In the matter of its penitentiary and convict camps, it is not necessary to
weary the eye again with figures.   Between the
dates of the last two biennial reports (1880 and
1882) a change of administration took place in
the prison management, affording, by a comparison of the two reports, a revelation that should
have resulted in the instant abolition of the Lease
plan at any cost.   Under date of October, 1880,
the penitentiary inspectors reported to the Governor that the contractors (lessees) had "provided
strong prisons for the safe-keeping and comfort of
the convicts"; that these prisons had "generally
been neatly kept," and that they themselves had
" required much attention to be given to the
sanitary regulations of them."   They admitted
the fact of considerable sickness at one or two
places, but stated that two of the inspectors had
visited the convicts employed there and " found
the sick in a comfortable hospital, with medical attendance, nurses, and everything needed for
their comfort."   They reported their diligent
attention to all their official duties, and stated,
as from their own knowledge, that during the two
years then closing the convicts had "generally
been well clothed and fed, and kindly and

humanely treated; and that corporal punishment
had only been inflicted in extreme cases." They
closed with the following remarkable statement :
" Notwithstanding our report shows a decrease
of one hundred and fourteen convicts, . . . yet
we think . . . the future of this institution is
brighter than its past." There had been paid
into the State treasury forty-eight thousand dollars,
and the managers in general were elated. But a
change in the prison's administration added a different chapter, and in 1882 a new warden wrote :

"I found the convicts confined at fourteen different prisons
controlled by as many persons or companies, and situated at as
many different places. . . . They [the prisons] were as filthy, as
a rule, as dirt could make them, and both prisons and prisoners
were infested with vermin. . . . Convicts were excessively and,
in some instances, cruelly punished. . . . They were poorly
clothed and fed. . . . The sick were neglected, insomuch that
no hospital had been provided, they being confined in the cells
with the well convicts. . . . The prisons have no adequate water
supply, and I verily believe there were men in them who had
not washed their faces in twelve months. . . . I found the men
so much intimidated that it was next to impossible to get from
them anything touching their treatment. . . . Our system is a
better training school for criminals than any of the dens of
iniquity that exist in our large cities. . . . To say there are any
reformatory measures used at our prisons, or that any regard is
had to kindred subjects, is to state a falsehood. The system is a
disgrace to the State, a reproach to the civilization and Christian
sentiment of the age, and ought to be speedily abandoned."

Almost the only gleams of light in these dark
pictures are these condemnations of the system by

those whose official duties require them to accommodate themselves to it, but whose humanity, whose reason, and whose perception of the public's true interest compel them to denounce it. This is again pointedly the case.

XII. IN VIRGINIA.

There the State prison has been for a long time managed on Public Accounts; but the management was only a mismanagement and a neglect; and when this came to be known, those in authority, instead of trying to correct the needless abuse of a good system, rejected the system itself and adopted the contract system. The report of the prison board for the year ending September 30, 1881, indicates that the change was made mainly, and probably only, on pecuniary considerations, and there seems to be reason to fear that this narrow view is carrying sentiment downward toward the Lease System itself. The board reports itself "pleased to discover, for the first time, that the general agent has reached the conclusion that the 'best way to make it [the prison] self-sustaining would be to lease the convict labor.'" At the date of this report the mischievous doctrine had already made its way through the Legislature and into the convict management; and the prison becoming over-crowded, a large company of prisoners were leased to certain railroad companies, beyond the control of the penitentiary

superintendent.   A glance at the surgeon's report
shows one of the results of this movement.   In
the population within the prison, averaging about
600, the death-rate was 1½ per cent.; while
among the 260 convicts on the Richmond and
Alleghany Railroad it was nearly 8½ per cent.,
even after leaving out of count certain accidental
deaths that legitimately belong to the perils of
the work and really should be included in the
count.   Including them, the rate would be 11 per
cent.   The superintendent does not withhold his
condemnation : " The system of leasing," he says,
" as is clearly shown by the statistics of the few
governments, State and foreign, where it prevails,
is barbarous in the extreme, and should be dis-
countenanced.   The dictates of humanity, if no
other consideration prevailed, should be sufficient
to silence any effort to establish this system of
prison management in Virginia."

XIII. IN ARKANSAS, MISSISSIPPI, AND LOUISIANA—
THE SYSTEM AT ITS WORST.

Even where the system enjoys the greatest
favor from the State governments whose responsibilities in the matter it pretends to assume, it is
rare that there is not some one who revolts and
utters against it his all too little heeded denunciation.   Such voices are not altogether unheard
even in Arkansas, Mississippi, and Louisiana,

where undoubtedly the lessees are more slackly
held to account, as they more completely usurp
the State's relation to its convicts, than elsewhere.
It is here may be found a wheel within this
wheel; to wit, the practice of sub-leasing.   So
complete in these regions is the abandonment, by
the State, of all the duties it owes to its criminal
system, that in two instances, Arkansas and
Louisiana, it does not so much as print a report,
and the present writer is indebted entirely to the
courtesy of the governors of these two States for
letters and manuscript tables imparting the information which enables him to write.   " The State,"
says the clerk of the Louisiana penitentiary, " has
no expense except keeping the building in repair."   " The State," writes the governor's secretary in Arkansas, " is at no expense whatever."
In Mississippi, the terms of the present lease
make no mention whatever of any moral, religious, or educational privilege, or duty.   " All
convicts sentenced for a period of ten years or
less, said lessees may work outside the penitentiary, but within the limits of the State of Mississippi, in building railroads, levees, or in *any
private labor or employment.*"   One of the effects
of such a rule is that a convict condemned to
thirty or forty years' service, being kept within
the walls, has fully three chances to one of out-
living the convict who is sentenced to eight or
ten years' service, and who must, therefore, work

outside.   Yet it is not intended to imply that the
long-term convict inside the prison is likely to
serve out his sentence.   While among a majority
of commitments on shorter periods, men, women,
and children are frequently sentenced for terms
of 15, 20, 30, 40, and sometimes even of 50 years,
a prisoner can rarely be found to have survived
ten years of this brutal slavery either in the
prison or in the convict camp.   In Alabama, in
1880, there were but three who had been in confinement eight years, and one nine; while not
one had lived out ten years' imprisonment.   In
Mississippi, December 1, 1881, among 77 convicts
then on the roll under 10 years' sentence, 17
under sentences of between 10 and 20, and 23
under sentences of between 20 and 50 years, none
had served 11 years, only two had served 10, and
only 3 others had served 9 years.[1]   There were
25 distinct outside gangs, and their average
annual rate of mortality for that and the previous
year was over 8 per cent.

During the same term, 142 convicts escaped;
which is to say that, for every four law-breakers
put into the penitentiary, one got away; and
against the whole number so escaping that were
but 25 recaptures.   The same proportion of

---

[1] From the nature of the tabulated roll, the time served by
those under life sentences could not be computed; but there is
no reason to suppose it would materially change the result, were
it known.

commitments and escapes is true of the Arkansas prison for the year ending the 30th of last April. In Louisiana the proportion is smaller, but far from small. A surer escape in Louisiana was to die; and in 1881, 14 per cent. perished. The means are wanting to show what part of this mortality belongs to the penitentiary at Baton Rouge and what to the camps outside; but if anything may be inferred from the mortal results of the Lease System in other States, the year's death-rate of the convict camps of Louisiana must exceed that of any pestilence that ever fell upon Europe in the Middle Ages. And as far as popular rumor goes, it confirms this assumption on every hand. Every mention of these camps is followed by the execrations of a scandalized community, whose ear is every now and then shocked afresh with some new whisper of their frightful barbarities. It is not for the present writer to assert, that every other community where the leasing of convicts prevails is moved to indignation by the same sense of outrage and disgrace; yet it certainly would be but a charitable assumption to believe that the day is not remote when, in every such region, the sentiment of the people will write, over the gates of the convict stockades and over the doors of the lessees' sumptuous homes, one word: Aceldama—the field of blood.

XIV. CONCLUSIONS.

There never was a worse falsification of accounts, than that which persuades a community that the system of leasing out its convicts is profitable. Out of its own mouth—by the testimony of its own official reports—what have we not proved against it? We have shown:

1. That, by the very ends for which it exists, it makes a proper management of prisons impossible, and lays the hand of arrest upon reformatory discipline.

2. That it contents itself, the State, and the public mind, with prisons that are in every way a disgrace to civilization.

3. That in practice it is brutally cruel.

4. That it hardens, debases, and corrupts the criminal, commited to it by the law in order that, if possible, he may be reformed and reclaimed to virtue and society.

5. That it fixes and enforces the suicidal and inhuman error, that the community must not be put to any expense for the reduction of crime or the reformation of criminals.

6. That it inflicts a different sentence upon every culprit that comes into its clutches from that which the law and the court has pronounced. So that there is not to-day a single penitentiary convict, from the Potomac around to the Rio Grande, who is receiving the sentence

really contemplated by the law under which he stands condemned.

7. That it kills like a pestilence, teaches the people to be cruel, sets up a false system of clemency, and seduces the State into the committal of murder for money.

8. That in two years it permitted eleven hundred prisoners to escape.

Which of these is its profitable feature? Will some one raise the plea of necessity? The necessity is exactly the reverse. It is absolutely necessary to society's interests and honor that what the Lease System in its very nature forbids should be sought; and that what it by nature seeks should be forbidden.

XV. EXCUSES FOR THE SYSTEM.

There are two or three excuses often made for this system, even by those who look upon it with disfavor and protestations, and by some who are presumably familiar with the facts concerning convict management in other States and other countries. But these pleas are based upon singularly unfounded assumptions. One is that the States using the Lease System, in whole or part, have not those large prison populations which are thought to be necessary to the successful operation of other systems. In point of fact, much the largest population belonging to any one prison in the United States, in 1880, was

in Texas, under the Lease System. The fourth
in numbers is that of Tennessee, also leased.
That of Georgia, leased, is more than twice that
of Maryland, managed on the Contract System.
The smallest State prison population in the
United States, that of Rhode Island, numbering,
at the close of last year, only eighty-one convicts,
showed a loss that year, on the Contract System,
of only eleven dollars. Missouri manages a convict population of the same size as that of Georgia, and boasts a cash profit, on the Contract
System. Indeed the State prisons under the Lease
System are, almost without exception, populous
prisons, the average population among the whole
twelve so governed being 920, while that of the
thirty-three that exclude the system is but 560.

Another unfounded assumption is that the
prisons working under the Contract or the Public
Accounts System receive their inmates largely
from the ranks of men skilled in trade. The
truth is, the strongest argument in favor of teaching trades in prison lies in the fact that men with
tradès keep out of prison, or appear there only
in decided minorities, in any community ; and
prisons everywhere receive especially but few
acquainted with the two or three or five or six
skilled industries that happen to be carried on
within their walls.

It is assumed, again, that the great majority
of the inmates of our leased prisons are not

only without mechanical training, but without mechanical aptitude. Yet, in fact, there is quite enough skilled work taught to just this class in just these prisons to make void the argument. Within the walls of the Virginia State penitentiary in September, 1881, under the Contract System, tobacco, shoes, barrels, and clothing were being made with a force of which three-fifths were black men. The whole force of the Maryland prison is engaged, within its walls, under contractors, in marble-cutting and the manufacture of shoes, stoves and hollow iron-ware, and in November, 1881, consisted of five blacks to every three whites, and of the entire number not one in ten was previously acquainted with any handicraft that could be of any service to him in any of these occupations.

Moreover, on the other hand, there is no leased prison that does not constantly receive a sufficient number of skilled convicts, both white and black, to constitute a good teaching force for the training of the unskilled. The Texas Penitentiary, in 1880, had on its rolls 39 workers in wood, 20 in leather, 50 in metals and machinery, 20 in stone and brick, 7 engravers and printers, and 11 painters.

The leased prisons, as it happens, have one decided advantage in this regard; the high average term of sentences affords an unusual opportunity for training the convicts to skilled labor, and making the best use, both pecuniary and reformatory, of their occupations. The South Carolina penitentiary is probably an exception ; and yet it is in this prison that the manufacture of shoes, say its officers, might easily be carried on with cash profit. In the Georgia penitentiary, in 1880, there were 87 sentenced for life ; 104 for terms above ten years and less than twenty ; 101 for twenty years ; 10 for higher terms up to forty years, and only 22 for as low a term as one year,—in a total of 1185 inmates. In the Texas State prison, in October, 1882, with a population of 2378, only *two* were under sentences of less than two years' length.[1] To increase the advantage, the long sentences fall with special frequency upon the class that is assumed to require an undue length of training. In the Georgia convict force just noted, for instance, only 15 were whites among the 215 under sentences above ten years.

But why need we linger to show that there is ample opportunity in these prisons to teach the inmates trades, if only the system were such as to permit it ? The choice of a better system does not rest upon this. In the Contract and Public Accounts prisons, it is not at all the universal practice to make the unskilled convict

[1] Some idea of the ferocity of these sentences may be got from the fact that 509 of these Texas convicts were under twenty years of age.

acquainted with a trade. This is done only in a few prisons. Generally,—much too generally,— he is set to some simple task, some minute fraction of the work of manufacturing some article, a task that he learns to do at most in a few days, becomes skillful in within a few weeks, and continues to do unceasingly from the beginning of his imprisonment to the day of his discharge. He works a lever or peddle that drives pegs into a shoe; or he turns down or up the rims of hats, or varnishes the heels of innumerable boots, or turns a small wheel that bottoms countless tin cans. He is employed according to his physical strength and his intelligence. It is no small misfortune to society that such industries leave the convict at last without a trade; but, comparing them with the tasks of the lessees' camps, it may be said they do not murder him, nor torture him, but are to those tasks what light is to darkness.

After all, these objections to the abandonment of the Lease System, even if they were otherwise well grounded, would fail at last when it comes to be seen that the system does not make good even its one poor profession; it does not, even pecuniarily "pay." In flush times it hands in a few thousands,—sometimes even a few tenthousands,—annually, into the State treasury. But its history is a long record of discoveries and rediscoveries on the part of the State that she has been the losing party in a game of confidence, with nobody to blame but herself. How much has thus been lost morally baffles estimation; suffice it to say, enough ungodly gains have gone into the hands of lessees to have put every leased prison in the country upon a firm basis under Public Accounts. Every system is liable to mismanagement, but there are systems under which mismanagement is without excuse and may be impeached and punished. The Lease System is itself the most atrocious mismanagement. It is in its very nature dishonorable to the community that knowingly tolerates it, and in its practical workings needs only to be known to be abhorred and cast out. It exists to-day, in the twelve American Commonwealths where it is found, because the people do not know what they are tolerating.

But is there any need for them longer to be unaware of it? There is none. Nor is there any need that the system should continue. We have heard one, who could give no other excuse, urge the unfavorableness of the Southern climate to prison confinement. But what have the reports of prisons in this climate shown us? That the mortality outside, among the prisoners selected (as is pretended, at least) for their health and strength, is twice and thrice and sometimes four and five times as great as among the feebler sort left within the walls. True, some of the leases still have many years to run. What of it? Shall it be supinely taken for granted that there is no honorable way out of these brutal and wicked compacts? There is no honorable way to remain under them. There are many just ways to be rid of them.

Let the terms of these leases themselves condemn their holders. There is no reasonable doubt that, in many States, the lessees will be found to have committed acts distinctly forfeiting their rights under these instruments. Moreover, with all their looseness, these leases carry conditions, which, if construed as common humanity and the honor of the State demand, will make the leases intolerable to men whose profits are coined from the flesh and blood of human beings. It is safe to say there is not a lessee in the twelve convict-leasing States who, were he but held to account for the excesses in his death-roll beyond those of prisons elsewhere in enlightened countries, would not throw up his unclean hands in a moment and surrender to decency, honesty, humanity, and the public welfare. But we waste words. No holder of these compacts need be driven to close quarters in order that, by new constraints, they may be made to become void. They are void already. For, by self-evidence, the very principles upon which they are founded are *contra bonos mores;* and though fifty legislatures had decreed it, not one such covenant can show cause why the seal of the commonwealth and the signatures of her officers should not be torn from it, and one of the most solemn of all public trusts returned to those official hands that, before God, the world, and the State, have no right to part with it.

APPENDIX TO THE 1889 EDITION

I.

THE TRUE SOUTH *vs.* THE SILENT SOUTH.

Burke said that no man could draw an indictment broad enough to cover a whole nation, but Mr. G. W. Cable has accomplished it in very brief space, in " The Silent South." One charge in substance is that the Southern courts and juries, not in a few scattered and occasional cases, but habitually and generally, prostitute their offices and perjure themselves to convict the blacks of crime ; that they affix a punishment, on the average, five times as great upon a negro as upon a white man for the same offence in the same courts ; that whereas the penalty for burglary is greater than for larceny, the courts indict and convict a negro of burglary who has only committed larceny, or, indeed, no offence at all ; and that these enormities are perpetrated in obedience to a public sentiment in favor of oppressing the negro.

That far more blacks than whites, in proportion to numbers, in the Southern States are convicted of crime is unhappily only too true. This must of necessity result from one of two causes ; either the blacks are the criminal class, or justice is prostituted and judges, witnesses, jurors, and people indulge easily and without scruple in perjury. Mr. Cable rejects the former solution and accepts the latter, and this in face of the fact that no man anywhere in the United States can be tried for felony without being furnished with a copy of the indictment and confronted with his accusers, and having the aid of counsel and the right to summon witnesses.

I propose to test the truth and accuracy of Mr. Cable's statements by official documents, which happily are at hand, and to show that he has made the grossest misstatements, to the prejudice of the Southern whites, in many important particulars.

He opens his indictment by charging that for larceny alone "such sentences are imposed as twelve, fourteen, fifteen, twenty, and in one case forty years of penal service, whose brutal tasks and whippings kill in an average of five years."

No such penalties as these are allowed by law in any Southern State, unless for a second offence. I have examined the criminal codes of most of them, and find that in Georgia, to which Mr. Cable particularly refers, the general crime of larceny is divided into: 1. Theft or larceny from the person. 2. Simple theft or larceny. 3. Theft or larceny from the house. 4. Theft or larceny after a trust or confidence has been delegated or reposed.

The penalties are: Horse-stealing—confinement in the penitentiary not less than four nor more than twenty years. Cattle-stealing—not less than two nor more than four years. Larceny from the person—not less than two nor more than five years. Larceny from the house —not less than one nor more than ten years.

Want of space prevents similar quotations from other codes in the South, but in none of them are such penalties allowed as Mr. Cable indicates, and it is not credible that any judge would venture to put upon the records of his court a sentence against a prisoner for a longer term than the law affixed.

Proceeding with the counts of the indictment in the order made, we come to this:—

" Larceny is the peculiar crime of the poorest classes everywhere. In *all** penitentiaries out of the South, the convicts for this offence *always** exceed, and generally double, the number of convicts for burglary. Larceny has long been called the peculiar crime of the negro criminal. What then shall we say to the facts, deduced from official records, that in the Georgia penitentiary and convict camps there were, in 1882, twice as many colored convicts for burglary as larceny, and that they were, moreover, serving sentences averaging nearly twice the average of the white convicts in the same places for the same crime."

Not only in the South, but everywhere else, burglary is regarded as a more serious offence than larceny, and the penalty affixed to it is greater.   But Mr. Cable says that the courts, the officers of the law, and the juries take advantage of this difference of penalty to send a negro to the penitentiary who has been guilty of larceny or some other inferior crime.   Fortunately, the records are accessible to refute this statement, and the examples of the two great States of New York and Ohio are sufficient for the purpose.

Official reports give the following facts on this point : That in the two Northern States of New York and Ohio there were eight hundred and ninety convicts for burglary and only seven hundred and seventy for larceny; and in the four Southern States of South Carolina, Florida, Alabama, and Georgia there were seven hundred and forty-seven for burglary and seven hundred and eighty for larceny.   In the Northern States quoted the convicts for burglary outnumber those for larceny and in the Southern States just the reverse is the case, and thus this count in the indictment is successfully refuted.

The next count states, "We are far from overlooking the depravity of the negro.   But those who rest on this cheap explanation are bound to tell us which shows the greater maliciousness : for one man to be guilty of hog-

---

* Italicised only here.

stealing, or for twelve jurors to send him to the coal-mines for twenty years for doing it?" I have already shown that such a sentence as this could not be rendered in any Southern State; unless possibly in a rare and occasional case, where the convict, after being once tried and sentenced, continued to repeat the offence, each time incurring an increased penalty. And the world—even its philanthropists—will not be inclined to think that a persistent and irreclaimable criminal like this is entitled to expect anything but the maximum punishment.

Next comes this from Mr. Cable's prolific reservoir : —

'In Georgia, outside of her prisons, there are eight whites to every seven blacks. Inside, there are eight whites to every eighty blacks. The depravity of the negro may explain away much, but we cannot know how much while there also remain in force the seductions of our atrocious convict-lease system, and our attitude of domination over the blacks, so subtly dangerous to our own integrity."

By this he means to say that courts and juries in Georgia send colored men to the penitentiary merely to afford a few citizens the opportunity of getting convict labor.

But if it can be demonstrated that in the Northern States as well as in the Southern crime is much more common and flagrant among the colored race than the white, and that in this respect the sections stand on a common platform, then Mr. Cable will be compelled to fall back upon the proposition that the black man and woman are more prone to crime than the white. Once more the official records are needed, and referring to them, and taking some of the leading States, both North and South, what is developed?

In the Alabama penitentiary there are about seven and a half colored convicts to one white. In Georgia the ratio is nine colored to one white. But in the District of Columbia, according to the census of 1880, there are 115,446 whites and 62,596 blacks, or nearly two whites to one black. And yet from January, 1881 (I quote from data given in the "Agricultural Review" for May, 1884, the accuracy of which I have verified by personal examination), to November, 1882, there were two hundred and fifty-three convictions for felony in the District of Columbia—sixty-four whites and one hundred and eighty-nine colored.

In the State of New York there are 5,016,022 whites and 95,104 colored people,—a proportion of about seventy-seven to one. But in the three State prisons of Sing-Sing, Auburn, and Clinton there are 2395 whites and 178 blacks—about thirteen and a half whites to one black. Or, to state it as Mr. Cable does, in New York, outside of her State prisons there are seventy-seven white persons to one black ; inside, there are only thirteen and a half to one.

In Ohio there are 3,117,920 whites and 79,900 blacks— a ratio of thirty-nine to one. In the penitentiary there are six hundred and three white convicts, and ninety-four colored—a ratio of six and a half to one. And in all the State prisons there were 1081 white convicts and 190 colored—a ratio of five and two-thirds to one. Again stating it as Mr. Cable does, in Ohio, outside of prisons, there are thirty-nine whites to one black ; inside, six whites to one black.

In the city where our national Government is located, where Congress is effusive in its care of the colored people, where Howard University bestows its benign influence, and in the great States of New York and Ohio, substantially the same state of things exists, as to the conviction of the colored race, as prevails in the Southern States. This being the case, there can be but one explanation : North as well as South the colored race furnishes largely more criminals than the white, and Southern courts, juries, witnesses, and people must stand acquitted in the minds of all fair men of the charges Mr. Cable brings against them.

It is in Georgia that Mr. Cable fancies he finds most to condemn. One of his main causes of complaint is that the courts inflict on colored convicts for larceny sentences five times as great as on white convicts at the same places. But the official report of the Georgia penitentiary and convict-camps for the period from October 20, 1882, to October 20, 1884, is conclusive on the subject. I took one of the penitentiaries, where there were five hundred and thirty-five convicts, and went carefully through the sentences for larceny, putting the whites in one column and the blacks in another, and then ascertained the average of each. I found the average sentence of the white convicts for larceny was actually greater than of the blacks! That for the whites was six years and one month, and for the blacks five years and six months.

The most cruel of all the charges which Mr. Cable has published against the people of the South is when he characterizes its penal service as one "whose brutal tasks and whippings kill in an average of five years." This is predicated specially of Georgia, but the official reports are once more available to contradict and disprove, in the most conclusive manner possible, this dreadful aspersion. Dr. Westmoreland, the physician having general charge of all the penitentiaries, reports that from the 1st of January, 1884, to October 20th of the same year there were sixteen hundred and thirty-nine convicts in all the penitentiaries, and during that period there were only thirty-eight deaths,—twenty-eight from acute or ordinary diseases, five from chronic or malignant diseases, and five from accidents or violence. This is really a low rate of mortality, and will compare

favorably with that existing in any city in the United
States, among the colored people. It is only twenty-
two to the thousand, while the mortuary reports for the
cities named below show in every case a greater percentage :—

Richmond	37 to the 1000	
Norfolk	34 " "	
Lynchburg .	30 " "	
Washington	32 " "	

Mr. Cable speaks of the mines at which some of the
convicts are employed, in Georgia, as particularly fatal
to life, and denounces the treatment that the colored
convicts receive there. But let Dr. Westmoreland and
Mr. Nelms, the Marshal of Georgia, tell the facts about
these mines. I quote from the report relative to the
Dade coal-mines. There were three hundred and
seventy-five convicts working at these mines, and from
January 1, 1884, to October 20, 1884, there were only two
deaths—one from cancer and one from accident. The
physician says :—

"The above table of sanitary statistics shows most excellent results,
particularly as to the mortuary list, as not one death has occurred from
ordinary camp or acute diseases—nothing, certainly, that could be attributed
to the management of the camps or their surroundings. One was killed
from slate falling on him, and the other died from cancer. These favorable
results, in my opinion, are due to three causes : First, to the humane and
intelligent management of the officers directly in control of the camps,— I
mean the physician and superintendent of the camps ; secondly to the well-
arranged and roomy prisons and hospitals ; and thirdly, not the least, and
perhaps above all, to the existence of a vegetable garden convenient to the
camps, of one hundred acres, in the highest state of cultivation, thus furnishing, the year round, that variety of fresh vegetables so essential to the
health of men in confinement."

And Mr. Nelms, the Marshal of Georgia, in reply to a
question asked him by myself as to the relative advan-
tages and disadvantages of the old penitentiary system
and the convict-lease system, answers :—

" Your second question is, Is the treatment of the convicts as humane under the present system as under the former penitentiary system ? I have no hesitation in answering that it is more humane. They have a great deal more outdoor exercise, they are as well fed, they are as comfortably clad, they are as humanely treated, and worked as moderately, as they ever were within the walls of the penitentiary, under the former system ; and being out in the open air a great deal more, their health is generally better, and they are more cheerful and contented than the convicts under the former system were."

The two races are nearly equal in numbers in the Southern States ; the blacks have the right of suffrage and all the other political rights that belong to the whites. Upon the conduct of the negro depends in a large degree the destiny of the white man ; and no one who is not given over to a blind hatred of the Southern white race can believe that they desire anything but the success and prosperous advancement of those who are to be their neighbors and coadjutors in the matters that interest both.

Mr. Cable imputes much "domination" over the blacks to the Southern whites. If he means this term as synonymous with oppression or wrong, I deny it emphatically. But the Southern whites are Anglo-Saxons, and in one sense that race dominates all others with which it comes in contact— red, black, or white. By virtue of superior energy and force of character they remand other people to a secondary and subordinate position. In this sense, and this only, does "domination" exist in the Southern States.

I ask fair and candid men everywhere to judge the Southern whites by official facts, which certainly afford the best tests by which to measure their conduct to their colored fellow-citizens.

RICHMOND, VIRGINIA.   JOHN W. JOHNSTON.

II.
A REPLY.

Ex-SENATOR JOHNSTON seems to me to be a very careless reader. In " The Silent South " I presented certain official facts which on their face appear to justify the complaints of the colored people that they do not get justice in court in the Southern States. And then I wrote, " Shall we from these facts draw hasty conclusions? We draw none. If any one can explain them away, in the name of humanity let us rejoice to see him do so. We are far from charging any one with deliberately prostituting justice." Does that sound like an indictment ?

The utmost I can be said to have charged I can condense here into an axiom : that nowhere on earth can one people hold another people in political or civil subjection, and forcibly monopolize the administration of the laws, without putting judges and juries into constant imminent peril of distorting justice. If an axiom is an indictment, what does the gentleman propose to do?

That he reads without due care is still plainer when he reports me as charging Georgia courts with "affixing an average punishment five times as great upon a negro as upon a white man," etc. I did and do say that for burglary the average sentence of the colored Georgia convict (1880-82) was twice as great as the white convict's; a statement the gentleman makes no attempt to refute. "This, too,"—I quote from " The Silent South," —" notwithstanding a very large number of short sentences to colored men, and a difference between *their longest and shortest terms* twice as great as in the case of the whites."

Neither does the gentleman attempt to refute this. Now the difference between the average sentences of white and colored convicts for *larceny* is almost nothing; but the preposterous difference between *lowest and highest sentences* of colored convicts for larceny was thirty-nine years, while in the case of white convicts for the same crime it was but eight years; and thirty-nine lacks but one-fortieth of being five times eight; which is what I say in "The Silent South"—a difference between their longest and shortest terms twice as great as in the case of the whites. "For larceny the [this] difference is five times as great." One has only to add this short, simple statement on to Mr. Johnston's first fine-print quotation of me, to see how unnecessary it was for him to have misconstrued its meaning; for that is its place in the original text.*

I shall assume that all Mr. Johnston's citations of law are correct; but when he cites the letter of law merely to follow it with the assumption that because the laws are so and so therefore judges and juries could not and do not pass excessive sentences upon colored men, I can only point him to the official reports of the prisons, and without venturing to impeach any one pray him to explain them away. He offers but one explanation, and takes no pains to make it good. It is merely his assumption that the heavy sentences of black men are in cases "where the convict, after being once tried and sentenced, continued to repeat the offence, each time incurring an increased penalty." Even this would not explain the gross difference between white and black men's sentences, for surely the reconvictions are not all and always black. But what are the facts? In the Georgia penitentiaries, October, 1882, there were 1243 convicts; 736 of the 1074 adults were under sentences of seven years and upward, yet only four per cent., 50, were reconvicted criminals.† One child

---

* See page 93. † See Biennial Report of the principal keeper of Georgia Penitentiary, October, 1882, p. 7.

of thirteen years was under a twenty years' sentence for burglary, and one youth of seventeen was serving twenty-six years for the same crime committed in the night. It is a confession of fatal weakness for the gentleman to appeal only to laws that prescribe what must be, and pass by the official reports that tell what actually is. If the laws say one thing and the prison reports say another, why are not the *prisons* called upon to explain? But in all this controversy the prison lessees are treated as tenderly as though they were honorable men engaged in a decent calling; and my critics spend their diligence to show that the cruelties officially recorded in these prison reports are fortified by statutes. Truth is, slavery and slave-holding fostered, and has bequeathed to the population of the Southern States, both black and white, a crudity and cruelty of criminal laws foreign to the humane spirit of the times. For stealing a horse a man can, under these laws, be sent for 20 years to a penitentiary, where in October, 1882, among the 218 convicts on sentence of 20, 30, 35, and 40 years, and for life, *not one had survived over 19 years of sentence*, and only four had lived out 17 years. There were then there 1126 convicts under time sentences, of whom 162 were under sentences of 15 to 40 years—that is, about every seventh man; yet in the whole two years preceding that date, out of 390 prisoners discharged only *two* had served 15 years of prison life, and none had been in longer. In Virginia, the *least* penalty for a larceny of fifty-one dollars' worth of property is three years in one of these penitentiaries.

Law or no law, the facts are terrible. In October, 1882, there were in the Georgia penitentiaries (among many others under higher sentences) 79 convicts under sentences of from only one to only three years for committing and for attempts to commit all the gravest and foulest crimes on the calendar. One ought to suppose, therefore, that for first offences in the various forms of pilfering called larceny three years would be deemed an excessive sentence; and yet, of the 216 convicts for larceny, only 37 were under sentence of less than three years, while 62 were serving terms of from 10 to 40 years. If men found guilty of murder—let the palliations be what they may—can expiate their fault in two years, how much or often must a poor wretch steal to deserve a sentence which no physical strength can live out?

It has not been my choice to lay special stress upon criminal affairs in Georgia. In South Carolina the law is, in one direction at least, more cruel than in Georgia. In my essay on the Convict Lease System a passage that to the hasty eye seems to apply to the Georgia prisons is meant, as a more careful reading will show, to apply to the system at large. The statement is that "Six men were under sentence for simple assault and battery—mere fisticuffing—one of two years, two of five years, one of six years, one of seven, and one of eight." This record really belongs to the South Carolina penitentiary for the year. I make these statements because I am an American citizen, and these things are happening in America, and are done by Americans in the jury-box and on the judge's bench. It is nothing to me that they happen in this quarter or in that, so long as they have happened and are happening in our common country. In other States of the Union the laws are less cruel and the prisons far more so. Mississippi, Alabama, and Arkan_ sas affix a maximum sentence of five years where Georgia imposes twenty, but their penitentiaries——!

The inference which the gentleman draws from the first paragraph of mine quoted by him in fine print is a false inference. As to his figures and mine, let us see: In the Maryland penitentiary, in 1883, the larceny convicts exceeded 260; the burglars were only 59. In the Eastern Penitentiary of Pennsylvania there were received, in 1884, 167 larceny convicts and only 49 burglars. In the Western, in 1883, the larceny convicts were 104, the burglars 35. In the Colorado State penitentiary, December, 1882, the larceny convicts numbered 118, the burglars 32. Of course, when a State has a number of correctional institutions, we must combine the statistics of all to find the true proportion between the numbers convicted of different crimes. In New York State, it is not enough to engross the tables of Sing Sing, Auburn, and Clinton; for the State has besides several other penal and reformatory institutions,—in New York city for instance, in Elmira, and, I believe, in Rochester; and these are just the sort to which culprits guilty of larceny would be sent to avoid throwing them into contact with the burglars of the State penitentiaries. The same is true of Ohio; but the same is not true of Georgia, though certain Georgians are making a noble effort to bring it about. In the Michigan State prison, September, 30, 1883, the year's admissions showed 71 larceny convicts against 35 burglars; in the same State's reformatory at Ionia, the previous year, the larceny convicts were 295 as against 44 burglars; while the engrossed criminal statistics of the province of Ontario for 1882 show the commitments for larceny 1401, and for burglary 63. I have not said that the disproportion of these two crimes in Georgia prisons extended to South Carolina and other neighboring States. For the gentleman to engross with the prison records of Georgia the prison records of other States with which Georgia courts and laws, judges, and jurors have nothing to do, merely to get a more favorable showing, is worse than

no explanation. And even if this were justifiable, ..e
does not by this device reach anywhere near a normal
proportion ; so, after all, he only drags the prison systems of these other States into the mire without pulling
Georgia's out.

As to the gentleman's misinterpretation of the second
paragraph quoted from me in small type: I do not
charge judges and jurors with consciously or maliciously
sending colored men to penitentiaries who should not
go there ; but I cannot take up the official report of any
prison where caste-rule and the convict-lease system
dominate without finding it full of facts and figures
whose accusations no Christian community ought to
leave unanswered for a day.   Look, for instance, at the
number of colored men and boys sent to these penitentiaries for slight offences; for when not even extreme
youth is saved from such cruel sentences as eight, ten,
fifteen, twenty, and twenty-five years for crimes against
property, and older men get even thirty, thirty-five, and
forty, it seems to me such figures assert that those who
are found in the same places for technically the same
crimes, on sentences of but one, two, and three years,
must have been comparatively trivial offenders.   And
when, on the other hand, I see in these prisons white
offenders against property serving *heavy* sentences,—
though not nearly so heavy as the black man's heavier
sentences,—it seems to me such figures imply that
white men steal and break and rob in those communities, and when the misdemeanor is great are brought to
even a cruel justice, if such a thing can be called justice,
but that when the offence is light the offender must be
dark, or the penitentiary gets him not.   Cruel implica-
tion! enough to arouse the indignation of any community! But whence comes it? From me? Nay, from
the official returns of the prisons themselves! In

October, 1882, the Georgia penitentiaries held under
sentences of only one, two, or three years, for various
forms of larceny, 62 colored men and boys and only
one white man. No wonder the black man's *average*
sentence for larceny did not exceed the white man's!

Or look at another fact. I am challenged on every
side upon the truth of the assertion that in 1880 a man
was in the Georgia penitentiary on a 20-years' sentence
for "hog-stealing." Yet *no critic ventures to consult
the official records.* One, who said he could easily consult them but who would not, produces instead the
following : —

DEAR SIR: I was principal keeper of the Georgia Penitentiary in 1880,
and there was not at that time nor has there ever been a man in the Georgia
Penitentiary under a sentence of 20 years for hog-stealing.

Truly yours,

JOHN W. NELMS.

Yes, John W. Nelms; from whose *official records* I
took the statement, and whose unsupported assertion
is worth we shall presently show how much. The
record is in his biennial report of October, 1880, page 45,
as follows : "Holmes Barry, colored, age 39, crime hog-
stealing, Jefferson County, term 20 years, received May,
1879." From Mr. Nelms's next biennial report, October,
1882, this convict mysteriously and utterly disappears,
not being reported as either present, dead, pardoned,
released, or escaped. Then in the same official's report
of October, 1884, he as mysteriously reappears as having
died in custody more than fifteen months *after* his disappearance from the previous record. And here the
poor wretch's record has been changed from "hog-
stealing" to "simple larceny"— from tweedle-dum to
tweedle-dee.

But is this case an exception or an example? By this officer's official rolls of 1880-82 there were two white convicts under the cruel sentence of ten years for "simple larceny." It is some gratification to know that no white man was serving a longer sentence for this crime. But the fact remains that under the same charge and at the same time 18 colored men were under sentence for 10 years each, 3 others for 12 years, 6 others for 15 years, and 4 others for 20 years; while one black man, William Williams, of McDuffie County, who was put in on a cumulate sentence for simple larceny at the age of 40, will, if he lives and serves out his term, emerge from the prison 80 years old. But this will not happen. These rolls show 406 convicts in the penitentiary under sentence of 10 years and upward; that is, one-third of all the convicts. The official figures show that these "long-term" men were coming in just 3½ times as fast as they were being pardoned and escaping; yet the report shows that of 380 convicts discharged on expiration of sentence, the proportion of these "long term" convicts to the whole number had dropped from one in every three to but one in every ninety-five. Death had made the difference. Not one was left to go out alive whose sentence exceeded 10 years.

The explanation has been attempted that these brutal sentences were given before 1868, and so antedate the convict-lease system in Georgia. But in fact, of the more than 400 long-term convicts surviving in the Georgia penitentiary in October, 1882, under 10 to 30 years' sentences,—many for simple larceny only,—*all but one* had been received since 1868; he the previous year.

One word in this connection it is pleasant to say: that in the Georgia Legislature there are gentlemen even now denouncing this whole convict-lease system as a disgrace to civilization and humanity, and nobly struggling to destroy it.* And like efforts are being made in every other State where the system exists. Would to heaven the same righteous and active war were waged by them against that spirit of race-subjugation which is the root of the whole trouble and the shame of our land.

Are Ex-Senator Johnston's efforts bent in the same direction? Far from it. His endeavor is to show that the "depravity of the negro" is enough to account for everything. But error has its uses, and the gentleman, instead of proving his case, actually brings forward an incontrovertible, arithmetical proof, based on official figures, that the "depravity of the negro" accounts for barely half. For see: In the District of Columbia, January, '81, to November, '82, the convictions were 64 whites and 189 colored. But the white population of the District is to the colored, as Mr. Johnston says, about two to one, or more exactly nine to five, and the *proportion* of convictions in equal numbers of white and black is therefore 1 white to $5\frac{3}{10}$ blacks. In New York State Mr. Johnston finds 77 whites to 1 black, and in its penitentiaries $13\frac{1}{2}$ whites to one black. This shows a proportion of convictions, in equal numbers of white and black, of 1 white to $5\frac{7}{10}$ blacks. In Ohio the population shows 39 whites to 1 black; its penitentiaries $6\frac{1}{2}$ whites to 1 black. The resultant proportion of convictions in equal numbers of whites and blacks is 1 white to 6 blacks.

Now, has the gentleman proved that in these regions "substantially the same state of things exists as to conviction of the colored race as in the Southern States"? He proves just the contrary. In Georgia the population

---

* In the Georgia Legislature, June 9, 1885, Dr. Felton said: "If the fiends of hell had undertaken to devise a [penal] system, devilish, barbarous and malignant, they could not have succeeded more fully than Georgia has succeeded in her system."

shows 8 whites to 7 blacks; in the penitentiaries, says Mr. Johnston, 1 white to 9 blacks, or more exactly 8 whites to 74 blacks; and the consequent proportion of convictions in equal numbers of whites and blacks is 1 white to 10½ blacks, *nearly twice what it is in the places with which he compares it.* Is it urged that the colored population North is a higher style of people on an average than the same South? Then let us turn to some region where the colored man has lately come from the South with all his squalor, poverty, ignorance, thriftlessness, and vices. Let us look at Kansas, the goal of the late exodus; what do we find? Population, 952,155 whites to 43,107 colored, or 22 whites to 1 colored. In the penitentiary, June 30, 1882, 504 whites, 113 colored, or $4\frac{4}{10}$ whites to 1 colored. Proportion of convictions in equal numbers of whites and blacks, 1 white to *less than 5 colored.*

And yet in these regions, where the proportion of penitentiary convicts among the colored race is but half what it is in some Southern States, it is freely admitted that the proportion would be still less were there not still a great deal of unreasoning prejudice against the black man on account of his color; while it is conspicuously in States where the freedman's consignments to the penitentiary are twice as frequent as his lower average moral condition will account for, that with the same mouth men justify race-subjugation and deny the warping moral effect of race-prejudice. Such is one of the foul fruits of slave-holding which it becomes the duty of every American—and especially of every Southern-born citizen—to help with all his might to destroy.

But one of the unpleasant consequences of acknowledging this duty is the necessity of replying elaborately to men who answer facts with crude misinterpretations, and deny the precious title of " Southerner " to whoever doubts the sacred dogma that the oligarchy can do no wrong.

Here, for instance, is Mr. Johnston's assertion that my characterization of the convict-lease system as one ' whose brutal tasks and whippings kill in an average of five years '' is predicated specially of Georgia. Not so. It is predicated of the aggregate results of the entire system throughout the South. In my essay on the con-vict-lease system I have spoken with specific accuracy of the mortality in the Georgia penitentiaries. I there showed that the official summary tables of Mr. Nelms, the State Marshal, whom Mr. Johnston quotes with such confidence, are not worth the paper they are printed on. The mortality in the Georgia prisons and prison-camps is not as bad as in some other leased prisons and camps. In the Texas wood-cutting camps, only a few years ago, half the average population died in two years. One of the habits of the system that screens much brutality is the lowering of the death rate by pardoning convicts whose health it has destroyed. In the two years ending October 20, 1882, there were 109 convicts pardoned in the Georgia penitentiaries, among whom more than half the number on time sentences had not served out half their terms, and many not a third or a fourth of them. Such a record is a record not so much of mercy as of criminal imbecility.

It is only as evidence against him and his kind that such documents are admissible evidence until these sworn signers of them have removed their implications by proving them false.

I repeat that as evidence in favor of his schemes or theories Mr. Nelms's reports are worthless. He reports 538 convicts received within two years; his rolls show 634. He reports 324 discharged; the list of their names makes them 422. He makes three separate statements that the number of convicts on hand is 1243; the addition is incorrect: the columns foot up 1193, and in the classification by crimes not a single number in the list agrees with the actual count of the rolls; while as to the total it is, by the rolls (which are not added up), neither 1243 nor 1193, but 1266   Everything goes to indicate that Mr. Nelms has not known for years how many living human beings he has in captivity, or ought to have. How is any one to know from such a source how many convicts have died that never went to hospital at all? The reports of the Alabama prisons are in a similar condition.   When convicts are in the care of men that make out such official reports as these, we need better evidence than their assurance, that the rate of mortality is low, and the more so when we know the frightful death-rates confessed by other convict-lease prisons, where, moreover, the rate is higher among the "outside" than among the "inside" men.

Mr. Johnston's comparison of prison death-rates with city death-rates, which include infant mortality and the like, is too absurd for serious notice.   Prison populations must be compared with prison populations.   The usual annual mortality of a well-conducted penitentiary is about 10 to 1000—one per cent.   Mr. Nelms, for 1880-82, claims this low figure without any foundation in fact. In reality his average prison population was 1266, and his surgeon's report for one year, August 1, 1881-82, was 22, or nearly 2 per cent.—nearly twice what it should have been.   From October, '78, to October, '80, the rate was nearly $2\frac{7}{10}$ per cent., which Mr. Nelms says is one-half what it had been in earlier years.   In the year 1884 the rate was over $2\frac{3}{4}$ per cent.

Yet this annual mortality, still nearly thrice what it should be when it had been reduced to half what it was, is one of the least offensive features of the convict management of Georgia, and one of the lowest death-rates known to this execrable system in any of the States where it is found. The death-rate in the Mississippi convict camps, 1881-82, was 8 per cent. a year. In Louisiana in 1881 it was 14 per cent. Such are the official figures of a prison system which exists nowhere among civilized people except where two centuries of slave-holding have blunted our sense of the rights of man. To quote once more my own words so carefully left unquoted by Mr. Johnston, " If any one can explain them away, in the name of humanity let us rejoice to see him do so." And let the ex-Senator make room for him, for he has only made the case look worse than it did before.

Only the necessity of maintaining the truth of my pages, brought into question by Mr. Johnston and others has induced me to lay the present statement before the public. I maintain, and have asserted from the first, that much of the injustice and cruelty practiced upon the colored race springs not from malicious intent, but from mistaken ideas at war with the fundamental principles of human right and American Government ; and the gentleman himself illustrates this by lifting up, after all, the standard of class-rule, race-rule, and status-rule, as against the right to *earn* domination without regard to race, class, or status, by intelligence, morality, and a justice that is no respecter of persons.

G. W. Cable.

III.

IS IT SECTIONAL OR NATIONAL?

Senator Johnston was right when he said Mr. Cable impeached a whole nation. If he meant, by his article on the "Silent South," an impeachment of the justice of whites toward blacks, that impeachment covers the Union from Florida to Oregon and from Maine to California. The same facts that are true from Richmond to Galveston hold also from Boston to San Francisco.

I base my assertion on a statement, by states, of the number of prisoners in penitentiaries, jails, calabooses, workhouses, military prisons, and the hands of lessees. Tables were compiled by Fred H. Wines, for ten years secretary of the Illinois Board of Commissioners of Public Charities, and are the most accurate of the kind ever gotten up by the government of the United States.

Figures deduced from these tables show that in the South * the percentage of the negro population who were in prison convicted or accused of crime was 3.67 times as large as the percentage of the white population so imprisoned. At the North the percentage of the negro population who were prisoners was 4.82 times as large as the percentage of whites who were prisoners. Thus on the hypothesis that judges and juries unjustly discriminate against negroes, a calculation based on the foregoing figures shows that Southern jurymen are thirty-one per cent. kinder to the blacks than Northern men are.

Taking only the ten cotton states and Virginia, the results are still more favorable to the South, and making the comparison within those states between negroes

---

* Under the title South we include the fifteen old slave states (with West Virginia), and the District of Columbia. The term North is used as including all the remaining states.

and native whites (the best basis of comparison) slightly raises the percentage of superiority.

In some individual states, both North and South, the apparent discrimination is very great. It is extremely great in Georgia, but *even worse* in Michigan. It is greater east than west in both sections, but notably so in the South. This is probably for the reason that the drift of the criminal classes among the whites is westward, which is not the case among the blacks.

Northern negroes are richer. They are less illiterate. They are more scattered and more subject to civilizing white influence and less to that of each other. They would also, naturally, be less hated, because of being few, weak, and helpless. These and other considerations would induce the reasoner to expect greater discrimination South than North. It would take a year's or rather many years' work to determine their mathematical value; but they may all be offset by two things. The institution of slavery implanted in the Southern negro temperance and subordination, a combination of qualities which the freedom of the Northern negro from any such school could never give him. Northern negroes are urban. Southern negroes are rural. There is more crime in cities than in the country. Hence we would look for the proportion of Northern negro prisoners to be greater. We have no statement of the division of prisoners into urban and rural, but an estimate reduces the thirty-one per cent. of greater Southern kindness to fifteen per cent. But, could all the elements of difference be mathematically eliminated, I doubt if the original percentage would be altered. The residuum of difference could probably be explained by the kind feelings of the Southerners toward their old slaves, and the fact that *their chivalry is rational.* They are favorably inclined toward *all* weak and helpless classes,

whether a weaker sex or race. Thus I think it has
been demonstrated, as near mathematically as such a
thing can be done, that *race discrimination in the
administration of justice is not sectional.*

In reality, it would be a miracle, under the circumstances, if absolutely no discrimination were exhibited.
As much of it as exists should be blotted out by our
vaunted "chivalry" and "philanthropy." Indeed, in
the North the negro is not protected by loving memories,
and justice can be secured to him only by repeated,
persistent efforts of noble philanthropists. In the South,
where the problem chiefly lies, there is certainly room
for improvement in the mutual feelings of the races.
The negroes are the wards of the nation, perhaps, but
each individual owes him the treatment due a fellow-
citizen and fellow-man. He owes this not only to the
negroes of a distant part of the country, but also to
those in his own state, city, or his own street. He owes
it not so much to those being tried before juries in a
distant state as to the men who come up before the one
on which he himself is impaneled.   *A. E. Orr.*

IV.

A REPLY.

Mr. Orr has, with great pains and accuracy and a
most praiseworthy deference to truth, drawn his conclusions from the Census of 1880, vol. i., pp. 3 and 929.
Yet his generalizing is crude. He says my "impeachment of the justice of whites toward blacks" "covers
the Union from Florida to Oregon and from Maine to
California." "The same facts," he says, "that are true
from Richmond to Galveston hold also from Boston to
San Francisco." Appealing to figures, he finds that in
all the Southern states the comparative criminality of
blacks and whites—if prison populations are conclusive

evidence—is less than four to one, and in the Northern less than five to one; the proportion being nearly a third *greater* in the whole North than in the whole South.

Now the first trouble here is that Mr. Orr is contesting a statement that nobody has made. In my reply to ex-Senator Johnston, my assertion as to an excessive disproportion of colored convicts is made only of "some Southern States," and specifically only of Georgia. Both there and in the earlier pages in which ex-Senator Johnston found this and kindred statements, they are to the effect that such things are actually occurring here and there and are *liable* to occur wherever the "attitude of domination over the blacks" meets the "seductions of the atrocious convict-lease system," which system, I wrote specifically, "does not belong to all our once slave States nor to all our once seceded States." Hence Mr. Orr is entirely wrong in resting his argument on aggregate statistics of the whole South.

But this is only the beginning of his error. He is wrong again in appealing to aggregate sums of *all prisoners;* for I spoke only of penitentiary convicts leased into private hands. So that the U. S. Census tables of all prisoners in jails, calabooses, etc., are not the proper data to argue from. The proper data are the penitentiaries' official reports. In South Carolina, by the U. S. Census, the comparative criminality of blacks and whites in equal numbers of each shows six and three-fourths to one; while the report of the State penitentiary for 1881 shows the proportion of blacks and whites committed to it over *ten to one.* Is this excess entirely due to an excessive criminality, or does not faithfulness to truth compel us to consider the additional fact that, while other confinements do not, the penitentiary does disfranchise?

27

I have not been so careless as to imply that even the convict-lease system works the same sort and degree of evil in all places alike. Varying conditions make varying evil results. This is plainly recognized in the seventh paragraph of my reply to ex-Senator Johnston and in other places in the general controversy. In Louisiana the disproportion of black convicts is not as large as in Georgia, and yet it has one of the most brutal lease systems in the whole South.

But do Mr. Orr's mistakes end here? By no means. He errs seriously if he would imply that I do not admit a greater depravity among blacks than among whites. The fact is palpable; the fault—we will not speak of that, for who would be innocent? In my reply to ex-Senator Johnston I said that gentleman had accounted for barely half the excess of black convict population attributed by him to "the depravity of the negro." And now comes Mr. Orr, and from another set of statistics accounts for the same five to one that ex-Senator Johnston had accounted for and leaves the same additional, remaining five to one without explanation in the states where it exists.

And still again the gentleman is wide of the mark when he says, "The same facts that are true from Richmond to Galveston hold also from Boston to San Francisco." They do not hold uniformly North or South, and only Mr. Orr has said they do. They fluctuate. There are regions where there is something like a general disposition to treat the negro as a man, regardless of race; as in Massachusetts, for instance. There are other Northern regions where—to quote my reply to ex-Senator Johnston—"It is freely admitted that the proportion of colored penitentiary convicts would be less were there not still a great deal of unreasoning prejudice against the black man on account of his color"; for example, in Illinois or Indiana. Again, there are Southern states, Tennessee, for example, where the proportion of colored criminality seems to compare favorably, not with such states as Massachusetts, but with such as Illinois or Indiana; though even this momentary advantage is more than lost when we leave census figures of "all prisoners," and turn to the states' own official lists of their *penitentiary convicts*. And, lastly, there are such states as Georgia and South Carolina, where the figures are simply indefensible Here is a small table of comparative figures:—

EXCESS OF BLACK CRIMINALITY IN EQUAL NUMBERS OF BLACK AND WHITE.

State.	By U. S. Census of all prisoners.	By State official reports of Penitentiary convicts under lease system only.
Massachusetts, ...	2¾ to 1	Convicts not distinguished by color.
Indiana, ...	6¼ to 1	" " " "
Illinois, ...	5⅝ to 1	5⅝ to 1 in Joliet Penitentiary.
Tennessee, ...	5 to 1	7 to 1.
South Carolina, ...	6¾ to 1	10½ to 1.
Georgia, ...	7⅝ to 1	13 to 1.

Mr. Orr's census figures are well enough, but his conclusions have an embryotic immaturity. He is not more to blame than a thousand others for overlooking entirely the figures of lynch law; it is the fashion to ignore them. And yet there they stand, in all their naked, shameless, unpardonable savagery. But passing them by, there is still between certain states this additional unestimated difference: that while in one the great majority of all questions of offence against

persons or property, small or great, are brought before
the bar of law and authority, in another the great
majority of such questions are submitted only to the law
and authority of one's good right hand. South Carolina will doubtless maintain its civilization to be not
greatly inferior to that of Massachusetts. On the other
hand, with three-fifths of her population of such sort
that the other two-fifths deny them full citizenship on the
ground of mental and moral unfitness, she will not claim
to be greatly superior. But in Massachusetts the total
of prisoners, even exclusive of reformatories, was in 1880
one in every four hundred and ninety-three of the state's
population; while in South Carolina—almost destitute
of reformatories—it was but one in every fifteen hundred and fifty. The total white prisoners in South Carolina, a State more than one-fifth of whose white population of ten years and upward could not write, were
only one in every six thousand nine hundred and eighty-
four. To assume that such a record indicates conclusively the amount of criminality in a population is too
preposterous for serious notice.

Such facts as these make it quite superfluous for Mr.
Orr or ex-Senator Johnston to find ingenious reasons to
account for excess of Northern over Southern incarcer-
ation of colored men. The North, the East, the West,
shall never find in me a champion of any error in them.
If I do not enlarge upon the presence of race prejudices
there, it is because I see their best people recognizing,
lamenting, and steadily crowding out the wicked error.
Moreover, I find but half a million dark sufferers from
this error in all the North. There are twelve times that
number in the South. Meanwhile I see in the South the
seat of the contagion, and her intelligent but deluded
people alternately denying and boasting its presence,
and openly proposing to perpetuate it, against the

peace of the nation and their own good name, happiness and prosperity. I have never yet spoken first in this matter, save under the conviction that silence was treason to the South. It is treason.

But I must be done replying to such critics as ex-Senator Johnston and Mr. Orr. Why will not some one for once attempt a reply to what I have actually said or implied? There are my statements; The Convict Lease System, The Freedman's Case in Equity, The Silent South; not one assertion actually made in any one of them has been even seemingly refuted. The false doctrines which so many have claimed to be the true sentiment of and right system for the South have thus far found no advocate able to speak to the point. I shall make no more replies to those who cannot; but if any can—there lies the gage in the open arena.

Mr. Orr seems to me the fairest-minded of any critic I have yet had. He seems really ready not only to acknowledge the truth, but to be in search of it. If he is he will presently find his way to an outlook whence he must see that this corrupting and execrable penal system distinguishes the majority of our Southern States from the rest of the enlightened world, and that the true duty of every Southerner is to make peaceable but inexorable war against it, as against all the foul errors bred in the South, and only in less degree in the North, by slavery.

George W. Cable.

ESSAYS ON PRISON AND ASYLUM REFORM

THE GRAND JURY:
A SAD PICTURE OF THE
PARISH PRISON AND INSANE ASYLUM

[From the New Orleans *Democrat,* June 30, 1881. Written by
George W. Cable, Secretary of the Grand Jury.]

To the Honorable the Judge of the Criminal District Court for the Parish of Orleans, Section A:

The present grand jury entered upon its duties in the beginning of April last. Much of its time has been occupied by individual criminal cases brought before it in the ordinary routine of court business. The results of certain special investigations have already been set forth in special reports. Other subjects of inquiry, as, for instance, the late action of the City Debt Syndicate in the purchase of premium bonds, after receiving much careful attention, were found to have been just and proper transactions, subserving the public interest.

According to established custom, the grand jury has visited various public institutions of the city and parish, appearing at these places unannounced and without previous appointment. In all cases the superintendents and assistants were found present and in the discharge of their duties, with such appliances and facilities as are furnished and under such rules of management as have been prescribed. A single matter of momentary but grave delinquency in connection with the scavenging system of one of the prisons was made a subject of immediate verbal complaint to the mayor of the city and was promptly corrected. There is, therefore, no criticism to be offered concerning the administration of the rules and regulations in these institutions, as they now stand, by the officials in charge.

The grand jury, however, feel compelled to report the system under which these managements are prescribed as being vicious in a high degree. In the parish prison the radical error is committed of making it at the same time a house of detention and a place of penal service. A common lot, and, still worse, a common intercourse, is forced upon the innocent, the untried and the condemned who come within its walls. An especially bad feature of this institution is the prison yards. In these criminals of all grades are allowed to mingle with each other and with those who, actually or presumably, are innocent of any offense and are only awaiting trial in order to resume their places in society. This common intercourse, moreover, is subject to little or no restraint but the rule of a so-called "captain of the yard," chosen from among the prisoners for the most conspicuous and irresistible ruffianly character. Cards and field sports are permitted, and loud singing, cheering, howling and indecent exposures of the person go virtually unchecked. In each yard the prisoners eat together. They are, in fact, isolated only at night when each is locked in his cell. The prisoners, whether serving out their sentence or awaiting trial for offenses which have not been proven against them, are obliged to do all the menial work of the prison; scrubbing of cells, galleries, yards, etc., washing their own clothing (or, oftener, their own rags), the removal of night vessels, etc. But it is probably unnecessary to go so minutely into the description of a system by which sentence begins to be executed before the prisoner is tried, and which is only and intensely brutalizing to all who come within its range.

Justice to the present criminal sheriff requires the statement that one or two highly proper changes have been made by him within the last twelve months. Before that time the sexes mingled freely in the prison yards. This he has put a stop to by bringing again into use a dilapidated quarter of the prison, which had long been abandoned.

The four divisions of the prison are now all in use. In one the white males are kept, without distinction of age, proof of guilt, criminality or sentence. In another are the colored males, boys of 11 and 12 in company with the oldest and most desperate criminals. In a third division are the colored women, more or less nude. In the fourth the white women are confined; and the utterly brutalizing effect of the place is evidenced in the fact that the white women are found in a condition of squalor and indecent exposure, worse than all the other inmates of the prison. Several of them were found almost entirely naked.

A well furnished dispensary inside the prison is now in charge of a young man convicted of a desperate and brutal killing. This prisoner has free access to the deadliest poisons, and, in fact, is in full control of them.

The well-known fact that the building is in a dilapidated condition need hardly be mentioned. There is not a breath of inoffensive air in the entire establishment. The stench of bats is stifling, and the odor of the prison is sometimes distinctly apparent a square away.

The condition of the city insane asylum differs only in degree from that of the prison. The part of the building in use is not so dilapidated; the ventilation is good; the place is kept clean and well surface-drained. The matron and her assistants are attentive and kind; the inmates are well clothed and well fed. Yet the institution is utterly unworthy the name of an insane asylum. It is only a jail for the confinement of insane persons, and is conceived entirely in the interest of the public comfort and not for the proper treatment, much less the care, of the insane. The system does not even theoretically comprise the attendance of a resident physician.

The city physician visits the place once a week. Beyond this, medical attention is received only — to use words of one of the keepers— "when somebody is sick." The liberty allowed the male keepers to go and come at will in the female wards demands emphatic condemnation.

In the face of such facts it is well to repeat that the persons in charge of these institutions are not accused of neglecting their prescribed duties. They do faithfully what they are appointed and paid (or not paid) to do. The keepers and nurses are, doubtless, as a body, conscientious servants of the public; but both in general culture and in professional training they are as ignorant of the real wants of the establishments and their inmates as these institutions are destitute of proper rules and appliances. In the insane asylum, for instance, it is purely from public neglect that the castaway barbarisms of close confinement and straight-jackets have not yet given place to the use of anodynes and intelligent discipline.

The blame is one which the members of the grand jury are free to confess their own share in along with the rest of the community, and they are convinced that no remedial measures can be made practicable before the public at large comes so to realize the revoltingly vicious character of the pres-

ent systems, that it will both countenance and demand the outlays necessary to the radical changes
involved in a better system.

Under this conviction the grand jury instructed,
and the mayor of the city requested, their secretary
to visit, during a leave of absence in the North and
East, certain houses of detention and asylum in
those regions. Visits were made by him to the city
jail of Boston, the State prison at Concord and an
insane asylum at Hartford.

Complete descriptions of these institutions are
not possible or necessary in this report, which can
only comprise in memorandum form a summary of
those features most worthy of imitation. The win-
dows and doors of all these institutions are so
situated as to preclude all communication with the
outside of the building, of every sort whatsoever,
while at the same time securing abundance of light
and air. The guard-rooms of the prisons are arranged so that one man, within a radius of about
five steps, can command a view of every gallery
and the front of every cell in the building. Each
prisoner is confined alone in his cell, a large,
thoroughly ventilated room. The menial service of
the jail and prison is performed with great thor-
oughness, celerity and quietness, under the immediate direction of an officer, by men who have no
intercourse with any prisoner, and who, for light
offenses, are sentenced to this particular service.

Although each prisoner is at all times entirely isolated in his cell, their careful classification according to sex and the nature of the crimes charged
against them is observed, in order that the stigma
of general criminality may not fall promiscuously
upon the various inmates. In short, the fundamental
principle of the institutions is to avoid everything
likely to lessen in the prisoner that self-respect
which lies at the root of all right-doing. Neatness
of dress, cleanliness and perfect propriety and dignity of manner is rigorously enforced. Bathing is
provided in a few small bath-rooms, whither prisoners are escorted in turn, as many each time as
there are bath-rooms. By a cheap and simple arrangement meals are furnished simultaneously to
all the galleries and distributed to each prisoner
alone in his cell. The whole number of attendants
is not larger in proportion to the number of prisoners than in our parish prison. Every quarter of
the buildings and every utensil employed is absolutely free from offensive odor, even of disinfec-
tants. The "night buckets" — of the same kind as
those so repulsively misused in the parish prison,
but of more portable size — are placed in each cell,
half filled with water, are removed instantly after
being used, and are themselves entirely odorless.
Duplicate sets are used. There is no water-closet or
earth-closet on the premises. Reading matter is allowed to prisoners in the jail, and is furnished in

the State prison; but in both cases it is subject to the censorship of the superintendent and must be of the most unexceptionable character. Padded cells, entirely inexpensive and well-adapted for their purpose, are provided for the victims of delirium tremens or persons of suicidal intention. The agent of a society for the care of discharged criminals is allowed to cultivate the acquaintance of convicts shortly before the expiration of their sentence, and under certain wise regulations those persons are provided with opportunity to begin life again in the outside world honestly and respectably. A remarkably large proportion are thus permanently reclaimed.

In reporting thus the more obvious merits of distant institutions, the aim of the grand jury is simply to emphasize the fact that there are beyond our State borders prison and asylum systems so superior to our own neglected systems, that in justice to ourselves as a community a thorough canvass of their merits and demerits should be made, with an eye to the reform of our home institutions. The more so as it is maintained by the persons in charge of these remote establishments that even they are still far from perfect.

The grand jury is compelled to confess that it finds its term of service expiring without having been able to give its attention to many evils which were called to notice and which seemed justly the subjects of public complaint. Inquiry into the merits of the case have convinced the jury that the creation of the office of chief of aids in the police department was directly opposed to the public interest and totally without excuse. The matter of bonds given in criminal cases is one which, the jury finds, requires legislation. Under the law, as it now stands, bonds, often forfeited, are never collected. Apparently the only remedy lies in giving them the character and full force of a mortgage lien upon the property of the bondsman, and requiring the proper officer of court to have them duly recorded. Any effort to institute that sweeping reform in the management of criminal affairs in this city and parish, the necessity of which has so long been apparent to the public and still more so to the courts, could not be better begun than by making practicable the collection of these bonds and the detention of witnesses likely, otherwise, to be beyond reach when wanted by the State. Several cases of this kind have arisen within the last three months.

The grand jury in April last recommended a cheap and effective apparatus for the protection of the public against the blowing out of steam boilers into the street gutters. During their term of service death has twice resulted from the absence of this or some similar provision, which could be made at an expense to each owner of such steam boiler of between $15 and $20. The jury again begs to call official attention to this matter. The industrial value to the community of the single able-bodied man whose life was lost in this way last month was more than the total cost of all the material and work necessary to have covered every dangerous steam discharge in the city.

The jury regret the necessity of turning over to their successors uninvestigated such noted matters as the hoodlum evil, the reckless use of clubs and firearms by the police, the abuse of the pardoning power, and others.

The jury takes pleasure in reporting the condition and management of the Charity Hospital, the Louisiana Retreat and the various orphan asylums, as in all cases excellent.

For the uniform courtesy and attention shown by everyone with whom they came in contact in the course of their duties, the members of the jury desire to express the heartiest thanks, and to make acknowledgment that several of the most decided evils and their probable remedies, to which they call attention in this report, were pointed out to them by the judge of this court, the mayor, the president of the Board of Health, the chief of police, the criminal sheriff, the district attorney and others.

In conclusion, the jury feels constrained to add its regrets that the reports of grand juries in general, and doubtless of this one with the rest, though they embody the conscientious labors of sixteen citizens, taken from their daily occupations to study the public interest for three months unrewarded, are destined to be heard and read but once and immediately consigned to oblivion. Against such treatment of matters of vital public concern, this grand jury begs leave most respectfully to enter its protest before this honorable court, the city administration, the public press, and the community at large.

Respectfully submitted,

O. HOPKINS
Foreman, Grand Jury

OUR VICE MILLS AND JAILS
FOR THE AGED AND INSANE

[From the New Orleans *Times-Democrat*, December 25, 1881.]

One glance at our Parish Prison, our Insane
Asylum or our House of Refuge ought to be, to
any informed and observing mind, a dreadful revelation. And it is. There may be differences of
opinion about every other branch of the public interest; there is none as to this. Concerning every
house of detention or charity, purely and entirely
under the control of our city government, there is
but the one conviction — that it is a disgrace to the
community. Debating the question, whether they
are worse than the worst elsewhere, is a pastime
rather too childish for the present progressive impulses of our people.

In the past, attention to these institutions has
been "everybody's business." Grand juries alone
have found it their duty by law, and have again
and again pointed there to the unbroken reign of
ignorance, inhumanity and neglect, and even of
personal scandal. But for this, matters might be
yet worse than they are; with this, we, the press

and the public, are enabled to build our present inquiries on the solid foundation of a candid, self-accusing admission of the truth in outline, and on the conviction that it is neither wise nor right to call these evils incurable.

First of all, then, as a community rising to a sense of its duty to humanity, to good order and to its own good name, the citizens of New Orleans should ask — and they are beginning to ask — "Why are these public institutions in their present state of disciplinary, moral and sanitary, as well as structural, dilapidation ?"

Is it because officials neglect their duties ?

The official points to the city laws and ordinances : "All these have I kept from my installation up. Do you see evils ? Point out the ordinances violated or else point out the correction. Am I," he asks, "paid to give myself to study, to research, investigation, comparisons, experiments ? Would you trust me with an appropriation ?" He thinks not.

The community draws off richer by at least the reminder that the matter does not require investigation, comparison, experiment, etc., and consequently, in one degree or another, some outlay beyond the poor hand-to-mouth, half-ration pittances which are all it is willing to entrust in the perfunctory hands of officials.

There is a chain of prescribed duties connecting

public officials with these institutions. There is another chain of legitimate requirements and just expectations in the hands of the people. One link only is wanting to unite the two and drag the whole public correctional and charitable system out of the mud. It is the same as that which joins the stockholders of any insurance company, bank, newspaper company or railroad to its salaried officers and clerks, and maintains confidence, and good grounds of confidence, between the two. It is a board of direction. No important scheme, commercial, financial, industrial, protective or governmental can prosper or expect to give satisfaction without it. And the late appointment of a prison and asylum commission, under an ordinance of its own framing, is emphatically the right step, and a very important one, toward the reclamation of those public establishments under the city's control, whose long and shocking inefficiency, even as but faintly explained to the public, has justly earned the complimentary titles given them at the head of this article.

How Not, and How, to Do It.

"Why a special board?" readers of the foregoing may ask. "Why not the grand jury?"

Because the grand-juryman, chosen blindfold from the public at large, has neither the necessary knowledge and experience nor the time to gather it. The momentary attention he can spare from the finding of true bills, etc., is but spasmodic and cursory. He points out a few obvious and superficial faults, makes his report, retires and sees it pigeon-holed. But when this special board comes to be a body of experts — as, in the way it is at work, it soon will become — then what a power for reform it will be, working with the grand jury!

"But why not a few hundred a year in the hands of the proper official, to be paid to professional experts?" Simply — one good reason out of many — because of the popular distrust of a one-man power and fear of a one-man interest.

"Then why not run these institutions by contract?" Because the universal verdict of those who are informed on the subject is that under such management all that is most desirable to be accomplished in such institutions languishes and mortifies.

"Well then by private benevolent bodies." No. They would be better managed than now, which, at most, is saying little. But what would this be save the simple, craven abandonment by the city of New Orleans, into private hands, of its plain duty to the merest decency and humanity. No private benevolent body could possibly qualify to take charge of the various sort of prisons, and none could be expected to take charge of the city's charitable institutions except under some species of contract : the least desirable of all contracts, since the management under it would invariably, in greater or less degree, take the standing of a work of beneficence and be free from bold and searching criticism.

The Board of Prison and Asylum Commissioners has a mountain of work before it, and it is the only power that, by the position it occupies and by the ordinance under which it operates, is thoroughly equipped for the accomplishment of the desired reforms. Its permanent efficiency is insured by the ordinance creating it, which makes it the bounden duty of the board to keep itself constantly and thoroughly purged of idle or indifferent members.

It will relieve no official of any duty. On the contrary, it is to be hoped it will afford such persons a new revelation of what their duties comprise. It will handle no public funds ; but where an official could procure one dollar of appropriation and satisfy the public as to its proper expenditure, the board will be able to procure ten or twenty or fifty. It will not legislate ; but it can carefully and faithfully consider and report what legislation, if any, is expedient and best. So, also, as to the management of the various institutions, regarding hygiene, sanitation, comfort, discipline, safety, the preservation of statistical records, corrective influences in the houses of detention, curative measures among the insane, proper architectural construction, etc. It will consult printed, and correspond with living, authorities and collect the best literature on all these points.

But added — or rather previous — to this, there is all the visitation, investigation and the like, on which this must found. How is the board — originally intended to consist of six, now consisting of fifteen members — to grasp the endless details of this task. Clearly not by increasing its numbers. As an unpaid deliberative body where dispatch is one essential, it is already large.

It was therefore from the first a part of this scheme to organize auxiliary to the board an association of citizens to comprise as far as possible all in our city, both ladies and gentlemen, who may be willing — if it be only to the extent of furnishing their names and addresses — to express an interest in these reforms. As explained elsewhere, nothing relating to it is or can become obligatory; but in this way the work may be expected, as it were, to take root in the community at large. From the ranks of such a body those will be found — though in no wise constrained — to give from time to time as called on by the board, their personal aid in committee work. Thus the work may be done, and those, possibly the majority, who are not disposed to undertake active co-operation will at least become the recipients of such reports or other publication as may issue under the auspices of the association.

A large number of names of our most prominent citizens has already been subscribed and is published in another column of this paper. During the present week copies of this list will be left in various prominent places, particularly in the different exchanges; and if the value, from every point of view, of a wise, humane and efficient management of our municipal establishments, penal, correctional and charitable, is as generally realized as it now seems to be, the number of names subscribed will hardly be limited to hundreds.

A PRISONS AND ASYLUMS
AID ASSOCIATION

[From the New Orleans *Times-Democrat*, December 25, 1881.]

The following paper has been furnished to the newspapers of our city for publication as part of a plan which is explained at length in other columns of our present issue :

It is proposed to form an association to promote a better public provision for the prevention and suppression of crime and misery in our city ; one that will practically recognize the duty of the community to see that all public correctional, penal and charitable establishments under municipal control are conducted in all respects according to the systems best calculated to meet on the one hand the highest requirements of humanity, and on the other the amplest protection of society; by the investigation and comparison of approved methods, by seeking proper legislation, by the education of the public mind, and by every sort of aid which can be offered to those who are officially invested with the management or oversight of such matters, to promote and encourage honesty and virtue among the neglected, the criminal and the indigent, both within and without our public asylums and prisons, and thus take away the blot that is universally recognized to rest on our city as to those institutions, and to make them worthy of the honest pride of an enlightened community.

It is desirable that the association include all who feel an interest in its objects, and it is understood that nothing further than this interest is pledged or indicated in this preliminary signing; that furthermore its constitution when drafted shall prohibit the assessing of members and the making of debts and insure the entire freedom of every member to decline all duties not convenient or acceptable.

Hugh Miller Thompson, A. Schreiber, Chas. E. Black, E. T. Merrick, Lionel C. Levy, Ed. W. Booth, L. H. Gardner, Thos. L. Airy, C. H. Parker, Samuel Simpson, Thomas G. Rapier, W. C. Raymond, ——— Gilmore, T. G. Richardson, O. Carriere, Conrad Kressner, V. Baudier, Wm. C. C. Claiborne, Jr., A. J. R. Landauer, Victor Meyer, L. Arit, E. L. Jeanrenaud, Theo. D. Miller, H. M. Weill, H. W. Lyon, W. F. Halsey, C. F. Hoffman, Cyrus Bussey, J. M. Seixas, A. A. Woods, Ed. A. Palfrey, Al. Hutchinson, E. B. Wheelock, O. Hopkins, W. H. Foster, H. Dudley Coleman, W. C. Shepard, Charles Gayarre, R. M. Walmsley, Louis Bush, John Chaffe, Wm. H. Chaffe, Herman Meader, S. W. Clark, Lloyd R. Coleman, John H. Kennard, W. W. Howe, S. S. Prentiss, H. G. Hester, E. A. Burke.

PRISON REFORM

[From the New Orleans *Times-Democrat,* January 8, 1882.]

In the first and second papers of this series, which appeared in this journal two weeks ago, it was maintained that an efficient prison and asylum system required a management on the same principle on which the business of all private stock companies is conducted; that is, by a corps of officers under the oversight of a board of directors.

This directorate is now furnished in the lately appointed Board of Prison and Asylum Commissioners.

The fact was pointed out also that the work before this commission of unpaid and preoccupied citizens is far more than it can efficiently execute, unaided from without. A project, part of the orginal scheme, was presented, for the formation among the ladies and gentlemen of our city, of a Prisons and Asylums Aid Association, to consist of as many members as there are persons desirous of seeing the proposed reforms set on foot, and involving no pecuniary pledge or obligatory service.

The Board of Prison and Asylum Commissioners, at its meeting on the 2d inst., passed the following resolutions:

Resolved, That this Commission adopt and recommmend the undertaking to organize an association of citizens to take an interest in the conduct of our prisons and asylums as assistant to this commission, and second the endeavor now making to obtain subscribers to the said association.

Resolved further, That the President be authorized to sign officially the list of subscribers to the association in behalf of the commission.

At the same time the members of the commission took in hand copies of the prospectus, for the purpose of securing signatures thereto. The number of signatures already approaches two hundred.

Let us now show more clearly two important facts:

1. That the prisons and asylums commission is the right kind of a body to co-operate with; and

2. That the public co-operation which it has accepted by anticipation is necessary.

The commission is a body appointed primarily by the City Council in the ordinance establishing it and defining its powers and duties; but it is perpetuated by itself. All vacancies are filled by its own selection, and the term of an efficient member may continue even for life; but either an active participation in party politics or inattention to the work of the board disqualifies any member and vacates his seat. Thus the capability and activity of the board is maintained, the benefit of long experience is secured, and it is rigidly separated from the machinery of political parties. A section of the ordinance creating the board makes the visitation and investigation of all the public institutions within its province, at least four times a year, an imperative obligation, and also requires an annual report to the City Council.

To show what the fulfillment of these duties involves will make plain the second fact — that the commission will have to have public co-operation.

Including the lockups, there are now placed under this board's oversight some twelve or more establishments scattered all over New Orleans, each of which is required to be visited and investigated once a quarter. That is about fifty such visits every year, or about one every week.

Moreover, it is right to assume that these investigations will be searching and exhaustive, and therefore cannot be made in the lax and hasty way common to grand juries, whose members content themselves too often with clean floors, whitewashed walls and a courteous reception.

Again, such work, to be effectual, must be done at unanticipated and therefore irregular intervals ; a feature which virtually doubles the labor.

Still again, it must be done, for the most part, not

in hours available for ordinary committee meetings, but by daylight.

We may sum up, then, 50 thorough and skillful investigations to be made yearly at irregular intervals, and in hours of business, by an unremunerated board of citizens pre-occupied in their private affairs and not relieved from the perpetual recurrence of these duties, save by death or resignation.

But, these investigations made, the work is but half done. There still remains the whole task of correction, involving inquiry after and into approved methods in all the various departments of these diverse institutions. And yet again, with each of these branches of the work there must be joined — if the board would secure either legislative or public support — the labor of making reports. Nor can we overlook the diligent study and research in many directions necessary in order to acquire a thorough knowledge how to make skilled investigations in each sort of institution.

It will be said that a board of fifteen should divide the work, say among five committees of three each. Undoubtedly something like this will be done. The most effective way and most economical, comparing the labor with the results, will be not a merely arithmetical apportionment of the work in bulk, but its classification under technical heads. Thus divided, it would fall, not to five committees, but to 10, most likely, and somewhat in this way : 1. Hygiene and sanitation. 2. Architectural structure, interior and exterior. 3. Prison discipline. 4. Finance and legislation. 5. Care and cure of the insane. 6. Vagrancy. 7. Juvenile criminals. 8. Friendless prisoners. 9. Discharged convicts — the latter two subjects found, where they have received attention, to yield results highly advantageous to society at large — and, 10. Statistical records, an invaluable branch of the work.

This rough sketch can doubtless be improved upon, but it is only an advantage that each member of the board would have to sit on two committees. The committees on architectural structure and hygiene and sanitation, for instance, would find it well to have at least one member common to both.

Now the board, so organized, would be able, and in justice to the work ought to, plan more work than it can possibly execute with its own hands. Hence, the Prisons and Asylums Aid Association.

The formation of an extensive roll of citizens under this name will make the reclamation of our prisons and asylums, as nearly as it can be made, a movement of the whole community. It secures an amount of individual attention which no other method would give. It supplies to the commission a distributing list for the issue of its printed reports, etc., with the best chance possible of creating a widespread interest in its work. It furnishes to the commission, in that body's efforts after the best

legislation, the wisest outlays and the most searching reforms, a many-voiced, yet intelligent and enlightened support, coming up from every direction
among the people.

No one will be bound to give anything or do anything, yet a general *attention* will be secured.
Among a large portion of those who are thus led
to yield attention, this attention will develop into
interest. And from among those interested the commission may safely take its chances of finding a
number who will volunteer to form transient special committees to execute small allotments of the
work planned by the commission.

This mode of operation is contemplated in section
6 of the ordinance, by which the board is required
to make or *procure* these investigations.

In planning such work the commission would
also prepare printed directions to be placed in the
hands of such volunteer committees instructing them
so thoroughly in the art of doing the work appointed to them that their execution of it would be
virtually the work of experts. Thus the work can
go on steadily year after year with the public interest in it sustained, the community better and better educated in these important matters, humanity
and the common good promoted in parallel lines,
vice and misery reduced and yet the burden of work
so distributed as not to fall too heavily upon a zealous few.

Let the individual citizen understand, then, that
it is only those who do not care whether our prisons
decrease or increase crime among us, or whether the
old Marine Hospital is an insane asylum or a mad-
house—only those who would as soon these institutions should disgrace us as do us honor—whose
names are not wanted. But that he, however prominent or obscure, who desires to see a blot removed
from the good fame of our city, and virtue, charity
and common security promoted, is solicited to add
his name to this roll; that nothing more is implied in
his signature, unless it be his own private intention,
except the desire of the commission to supply him
with their publications, trusting that he will read
them.

No space is left here to point out the need of both
ladies and gentlemen in this work. Most persons
will see it at a glance. In many institutions there are
female wards, which only ladies can successfully
investigate. Other branches of work only men can
grasp. There are parts of our country where half
the good work done in this direction is accomplished
by women. The other half is necessarily done by
men.

As indicative of the present condition of one of
the institutions in which reform is called for, we
may note the report of the City Insane Asylum for
1881, published in THE TIMES-DEMOCRAT of
the 5th inst. The year opened with 162 inmates.

The new admissions during the year numbered 169, and the releases—*releases* is good!—amounted to 140. To those acquainted with the statistics of insane institutions it goes without saying that the "releases" were, in great part, from among the new admissions, and that, as a consequence, the mortality must have been principally among the older inmates. But to make sure of being more liberal than we need be, we may assume 200 patients to have spent considerable portions of the year in the asylum. Out of this number, then, how many died? Sixty-nine. No plague that ever visited this continent ever swept off such a year's ratio of mortality. No city whose health records show a death-rate of 3 per cent a year can claim to be called a healthy city. The rate in New Orleans has for some years been in the neighborhood of 2½. Twelve or 15 per cent is not a low rate for a hospital. The percentage of mortality in a well-ordered insane asylum, whose report for 1880 lies before the writer, is thirteen. But among the inmates—able-bodied and all—of our jail for the insane the year's mortality is more than every third person. And it has *no resident physician.*

Now if it can be shown — as it certainly can be — that there are twenty other features of our public institutions as bad as this one, ought not almost everybody to feel an interest in seeing them reformed? It looks so.

A ROGUES' CONGRESS

[From the New Orleans *Times-Democrat,* January 22, 1882.]

In one of our large cities there is now in session a general assembly of rogues from all parts of the country, and from many foreign lands. In this body may be seen the representatives of every vicious class : Counterfeiters, tramps, sneak-thieves, house-burners, stage-stoppers, town-vagrants, murderers, poisoners, common drunks, pick-pockets, burglars, defaulters, ravishers, embezzlers, wharf-rats, bandits — what you will.

The excuse for the existence of this body is — the reduction of crime ! Its meetings are held daily from sunrise to sunset, in a large paved court, shut out from the public eye on every side by a cordon of lofty buildings. The total of its delegates in the three or four groups into which it is divided often exceeds 300. The order is only what might be expected. There is no little congeniality among its members, and their deliberations are characterized by some mirth and noise which, at certain intervals, rise into concerted howlings as signals for the introduction of this or that business of the day.

There are no desks, chairs or benches. The members attend *en costume,* and the display of rags and tatters, and much noticeable nakedness, is a prominent feature. The stench of the place is another.

Without that show of method which deliberative bodies commonly display, they yet accomplish all the ends of executive sessions, committees, conferences, debates, personalities and contests for the floor — or pavement. The head of this body is one of its own number, chosen for his superlative strength and ferocity, which qualities he uses to enforce his enlightened ideas of decency and order.

The graduates of this school, after terms of training, varying in length from five days all the way up to numerous months, are sent out with their diplomas written on their hearts and foreheads, and are scattered broadcast in the streets and hiding places of the city, among the towns and villages of the State, and far out along the highways and by-paths of other States, and into the darkest retreats of vice in other cities.

What business is concocted here is known to law-abiding folk only inferentially, and each present reader must be left to his individual guessing powers; but it would be shorter work, no doubt, to name the crimes not devised here, provided there be at least one with which to begin the enumeration. Like many other collective bodies, its members come and go singly or by installments, the whole number never being all old or all new, and the analogy is continued in the fact that some of its members go and come again repeatedly.

It will be seen, then, that this institution must be also a school; a public school, sustained at the expense of the city and State, boarded and lodged by the one and officered and guarded by the other. As an establishment for the acquisition of certain accomplishments, its efficiency is very near perfection.

But what State or city is it that can afford to allow itself this hideous luxury?

It is our own city of New Orleans, which, in its Parish Prison, combines in one a rogues' congress and a high-school of vice.

Instead of diminishing crime, all the tendencies of the concern are to increase it. If it were anything like an approved modern institution, not making new experiments, but merely comprising such features as have been found to bring good results wherever adopted, it would reduce the amount of vice and crime with which it has to do, and would not be at the same moment a moral nuisance and a disgrace.

It would be either a house of detention for persons awaiting criminal trial or a place of penal sentence for condemned criminals. It would in no case be deemed allowable to make it both in one. If it were a simple jail for the untried then each inmate would be kept in his cell, where he would be supplied with all that is decently due to one upon whom as yet, being untried, no punishment can fall : a cot, sufficient bedding, a clean, dry, well ventilated cell, a chair, stool or bench and a sufficiency of plain, wholesome food. Luxury and cruelty would alike be rigidly excluded. The whole arrangement would be a recognition of the fact that, be the prisoner innocent or guilty, society could only lose by each and every act of injustice or oppression practiced upon him or her before trial. The community would, in the merest self-protection, carry out the principle that in administering justice it must itself be just.

On the other hand, the ground of detention is the necessity of assuming that the prisoner may be guilty of the crime charged. Then he certainly should not be allowed, for any part of day or night, to herd with other criminals. He would be confined in his cell alone, and not allowed in any way to communicate with any other prisoner. If our Parish Prison were a well-ordered house of detention, no prisoner would ever see the face of another. Our rogues' congress would be prorogued, *sine die.*

"Where is your prison yard?" said the present writer to the jailer in the central prison of a distant city.

"Prison yard?" The man could not understand. "Prison yard? What ! A place for prisoners to roam around and talk to each other in, to concoct new villainies in, which will be put into effect directly they are out, to plan escapes, to stimulate each other with vicious braggadocio, to communicate each other's vices and vicious arts each to all, to make a larger gathering of lawbreakers than they would dare attempt to make in a state of freedom — a fouler den of vice than any that our police has ever broken up? No, we have no prison yard."

The visitor from New Orleans was tempted — but that was not the time and place to speak, and for the honor of his town he remained silent — was tempted to say to the jailer:

"Monsieur Jailer, you don't know everything. You've never seen our Rogues' House of Congress, down yonder. We have it divided like this jail—into departments. You have one wing for females, another for petty male offenders, a third for men under graver charges. We have four divisions. These have nothing to do with the question of the degree of criminality involved in the charges. First, we divide males and females, making two divisions; then we separate whites and blacks; we are very particular about that, and that makes four. Each class has its gallery of cells and its common yard. The cells stand open all day. All ages, sometime even down to childhood, and all degrees of viciousness and depravity and brutality — from a lad who has stolen $5 out of a carelessly kept till, to a man who has killed his wife with an ax — swarm and companion together. In the male yards men strip naked in the open air at will and souse themselves into a huge tank of water. A 'captain of the yard,' chosen for his transcendent brutality, often the principal in some horrible murder, holds sway over the rest. Prisoners are taken out every day, brought into court and acquitted of all charges against them whose every moment's experience within its walls is a brutal punishment to any but an utter beast.

"Women are seen there in their open yards with nothing on them but a thin and tattered shift, moving shamelessly before the eyes of the male keepers or of visiting grand jurymen. You would, in all likelihood, the time being midsummer, see one or two women, white or black, stark naked in their cells. These women, having no bath-tub, strip naked at night and get under the hydrant in the open yard. The black women, having not even a hydrant, carry water from the white women's hydrant in wooden night-soil buckets — a little the filthiest things that were ever called utensils — and wash in them.

"The cells are clean to the eye—because the prisoners themselves, male or female, guilty or not guilty, have to clean them, but they are foul to the nostrils, and without seats or beds or anything but a blanket and a floor. The stench of that prison can be smelt a hundred yards away. It is hard to tell whether its liberties or its cruelties are the more utterly brutalizing."

There is more to be told — truths that would soil

this page and make it unreadable. But is not this enough? The writer did not think best to say these things abroad. But is it not our duty to know them at home?

The prisons and asylums commission are at work. It was intended to give in this article a summary of their movements. Their reports lie at hand for this purpose; but for the second time this summary is crowded out for want of space. It is proposed this week to give the Prisons and Charities Aid Association organized form. It will be well, in doing so, to have as many citizens on its rolls as can be secured. These rolls are in the hands of several persons. Nothing is asked but the moral support of each citizen's name. Can any one refuse that?

Meantime the board of commissioners does not wait, but works. As yet it is operating only on the surface. Probably they cannot do more until the public — the whole public — is aroused to the universal shame and the universal damage of supporting such institutions as our Rogues' Congress, and shall demand that its members be locked in their cells, and the prison yards abolished once for all. Then we can turn to the reform of fifty other abuses only less abominable.

OUR MAD-HOUSE
DEATH-RATE EXPLAINED

[From the New Orleans *Times-Democrat*, February 5, 1882.]

It is strange, but it is true, — a community will commit crimes which, if commited by one man, would be so abhorred by it that jail walls would hardly protect him from the fury of the people.

Public institutions are sometimes an example. An ill-managed public institution — at least in our free country — is the incessant crime of the whole community.

Here is our City Insane Asylum. The terrible outrage committed only a few months ago in that establishment certainly could never have gone unpunished but for the consciousness of the community that in the guilt of that transaction it had a lamentable share, which it was not prepared to wipe out. It was our duty to humanity and to our own good name to have had an insane asylum in fact; one in which such a deed would have been impossible. But this act was only a momentary evidence of a constant condition.

The community will not always rest easy under

this burden of culpability. Having all this while recognized the truth that the indigent insane must be provided for, it will some day realize the duty and — economy — pardon the word — of making proper provision. Why not now? Why not to-day? What are the facts necessary to be practically recognized?

First, this: That "in its earliest stages insanity is a very curable disorder." The common practice among us now is to keep an insane person out of the asylum until his friends are afraid of him. "The statistics of all asylums are as one in proving that the more recent the outbreak, the better is the chance of recovery; the expectation whereof indeed is about four to one where efficient treatment has been put in force within three months from the commencement of the disease, but hardly as much as one in four when it has lasted 12 months." "Nothing is more true or clear than that a very large proportion of the insane recover the perfect use of their understanding." "Few popular errors are more prejudicial to the interests of humanity than that insanity is, commonly, incurable; and, consequently, that the application of remedies is superogatory."

The certainty of good results points as straight as a sunbeam to our plain duty toward the indigent insane; it is their cure, not merely their confinement.

But the demands of the public purse are in the same direction. It is not the cure of new, but the non-cure and detention of old cases that makes the asylums cost. The best and earliest treatment is the cheapest. "True economy," says an authority, "as well as humanity requires that provision for the insane should be ample and well devised, with a view to the relief of the public from the necessity of their support." "It is," says Mortimer Granville, "a question of hours; days are as months and years in this emergency. The three days allowed by the law before a relieving officer brings a case before a magistrate costs the country (England) annually enough to maintain a large asylum."

Now, what is it, so priceless, and at the same moment so economical, which the well-appointed asylum secures to its inmates? Very simple things, but which only experts and the proper appliances can furnish; by day, tranquility, appetite, suitable food, bodily comfort, occupation, exercise, amusement; by night, the "sweet restorer," sleep; and day or night, constant professional oversight and a kind and skillful moral influence and control. Also retirement, when retirement is best; sociability when that is best; books, pictures and flowers, the three cheapest things on earth; and a careful classification and separation of different grades of insanity, in order that these may not chafe one upon another.

All these are good, the most of them essential.
"The importance of securing regular and sufficient
sleep cannot * * be too strongly insisted on. Every
effort should be made to obtain its conditions for
every lunatic. Comfortable quarters, quiet nights,
unbroken by any agitating occurrences or noises,
are among the essentials to this end." "In all these
asylums where the dietary is not liberal, there the
recoveries are few, and the deaths many; and on
the other hand, in those institutions where the dietary is ample, there the proportion of recoveries and
deaths in reversed," etc.

In good asylums all these conditions are found.
Peace, quiet, order, beauty and comfort reign there
supremely and continuously, night and day, in the
perfection of a model home unvisited by affliction
or discord. And this, we are told, is the cheapest.
Let us pause and think of that!

Our space is being consumed, but before it is all
gone let us see whether our asylum supplies these
desiderata.

It stands out on an open, desolate, half-drained
plain that was once a cypress swamp. The grounds
within its high, rough plank fence are of an aspect
only a little less melancholy than that without. On
entering the gateway a broad porch comes to view
on which a number of unoccupied female insane at
once begin an excited demonstration, lifting their
arms, spreading their fingers, and grimacing. He

finds the few large apartments into which the female ward is divided, totally unfitted, by their arrangement, for the proper oversight of the inmates. These unfortunates roam about from one apartment to another restlessly, disturbing and exciting each other, with ill-trained female attendants and ignorant male keepers moving at will among them. As the visitor passes through he sees wild gesticulations, stealthy approaches, startled retreats, scampering hither and thither; is accosted by this lunatic and that, begged for tobacco and for liquor, rallied with loud outcries, sudden quarrels, loud laughter and the foulest obscenities; the poor creatures gibber, and mutter, and peep through the cracks of doors or around corners; frequently one falls to tormenting another, and every few moments there is a general hubbub. They are clothed in harsh, rough garments, that to the over sensitive skin of many insane is a perpetual and excruciating torture. In short, in this so-called asylum for a class of unfortunates whose every sensibility is exquisitely sharpened by disease, there is not a moment of true tranquility in the day. Tranquility! appetite! comfort! amusement! occupation! well, yes, a few quiet ones do sit and sew — when they are quiet; but exercise! amusement! retirement! There are no answers.

"But," says a keeper, "If you think this is anything, you ought to hear them at night."

"Pretty bad at night, is it?"

"O, it's just hell!"

There is no classification of patients according to degrees of ailment. The chronic insane and the acute (new) cases—two classes that in some countries are not allowed to occupy even the same asylum — are thrown into actual contact; the epileptic, the seemingly rational, the lunatic, the idiotic, each inmate receiving all the damage derivable from the insanity of the rest. No wonder they die rapidly!

The "dangerous," it is true, are confined — a treatment condemned by the highest authorities — kept in what are nothing more or less than wooden cages. The long abandoned straight-jacket and shower-bath discipline are in habitual use. The violent are thrown into cells where they often knock themselves about in a fearful manner and defile the place and their own persons most revoltingly. Women who have moved in good society, who are lady-like and still retain fair degrees of intelligence and sensibility are thrown into company with idiots and with women of the vilest renown, whose mouths are still an open sepulchre and whose aliases are familiar to every reader of police records.

The writer one day saw, in the male yard of this institution, a man standing and blinking straight into the sun. His face was inflamed and his eyes seemed well nigh burned out of their sockets. It was his mania to stand in one spot and look at the sun from morning till night, and he was simply allowed to do it!

The following conversation actually took place:

"Who is the physician of this establishment?"

"The City Physician."

"How often does he come here?"

"Whenever anybody is sick."

— As if anybody there were well!

Every inmate that enters that house of horrors is virtually, from the very conditions into which he is thrown, an "incurable"; those who recover would have recovered sooner outside; and the institution which is a blasting disgrace to us costs us less than one that would do us honor — if it does cost less — only by reason of the terrible death rate which its condition and management inflicts upon its inmates.

Such institutions are alluded to by writers on the subject to-day only as the discarded and vanished barbarities of other ages. England is 50 years, France a hundred ahead of this. And yet, at least until lately, rumor has been rife, of an inside history of this establishment that would cast this surface view into eclipse and bring the blush to the cheek of a murderer.

How many more carnivals shall we have before we remove this foul blot?

Authorities quoted:

Pathology of the Mind, by Henry Maudgley, M. D., New York: 1880.

Care and Cure of the Insane, by J. Mortimer Granville, M. D., F. R. S., etc. London : 1877.

Burrows (*Inquiry,* etc., 1820), as quoted by Mortimer Granville.

Publications No. 12 and No. 22 of the State Charities Aid Association of New York.

HOW TO INSPECT A PRISON

[From the New Orleans *Times-Democrat*, February 19, 1882.]

There is one principle for which a prison stands as a dark and silent index — Justice. This is the iron key that locks the prisoner in and lets him out.

To be minutely exact, it might be said that prisoners are an index of man's endeavor after justice. And since mankind, all, must couple themselves by the frailty of their natures, unjust, common protection alone can justify them for attempting to administer justice upon the individual.

Hence the place of all places where injustice is most utterly without defense is within the walls of a prison.

It is, moreover, disastrous. If prisoners are to be let out again after a term either of sentence or of mere detention, it is, without doubt, grossly against the interests of society and the State that these late captives should come back to their former lives outraged with a sense of injustice practiced upon them, and convinced that human justice is only injustice after all. Whether they are to be let out or not, the same dangerous effect spreads to their relatives and friends.

The keynote, therefore, to all investigation of a prison is the principle of justice. Whether the immediate question be one of punishment or of discipline, of safe custody, food and clothing, personnel of official staff, reformation of prisoners or construction of buildings, no other consideration can rightly or safely take precedence of justice. It is the very cement that holds stone to stone, and without it any prison ought to tumble down, having actually less right to exist without it than the courthouse has.

Justice secured, the next imperative principle is economy. Human society erects prisons only because its bad members compel it to do so. It is therefore justified in practicing, regarding them, a close economy. And beyond the demands of simple justice, nothing inconsistent with the closest economy can be claimed. All that society or the State may choose to add to this is founded in expediency. And this, expediency, is the third necessary idea.

The questions, therefore, to be settled concerning every detail of intention, construction, or management in and about a prison, are these and in this order : 1, is it just? 2, is it economical? 3, is it expedient?

The question of economy falls in the middle. It is neither fundamental nor final, and depends, in every case, on the affirmative answer of the other two. Nothing is cheap that is unjust or morally inexpedient.

Persons are imprisoned for one or more of three objects: safe-detention, merely; punishment; reformation.

The protection of society requires the prisoner's safe custody. It does not require, but forbids, since justice forbids, everything avoidable that endangers the prisoner's life, limb or health, and as long as he be unconvicted, everything which resembles punishment, not demanded by safe conduct or economy.

If the prisoner be a convict, then the protection of society requires that his sentence be clearly defined and exactly executed; and it does not require, but forbids that it be in any degree taken from or added to by any hardship, pain, ignominy, risk or privilege not contemplated in his sentence.

If the prisoner is kept for reformation, it is because the measure has been decided upon as one of expediency, and the questions to be investigated as to its details are simple, those of expediency and efficiency. That reformatory discipline is highly expedient even with adults, we need not pause to say. That it has been made efficient statistics prove.

Coming down to practical details, the work of investigation is suddenly simplified when it is seen that justice and expediency are found to run directly upon the line of economy. Bad prisons are without excuse; they cost the most.

Take the single item of safe custody: The modern plan of the perpetual oversight of the prisoner costs a trifle, compared with the old system of immense, impenetrable walls, which, yet, were never certainly impenetrable.

Let us throw together, without pretension of completeness, a list of inquiries to be made by one investigating a prison, and of facts to be reported by him.

1. Is there in use a set of printed rules defining clearly, completely and properly the duty of each kind of officer, employe, domestic and prisoner?

2. Are these rules properly made known to all, and are they always rigidly enforced?

3. Does careful and ingenious questioning in various directions indicate that such is the fact?

The inability to answer yea to these three questions is *prima facie* evidence of a bad prison.

4. Do the books of the prison, after scrutiny, seem to be so kept as to make frauds or errors, as nearly as may be, impossible?

5. Are the safeguards against fire and surprise adequate, and what are they?

6. Are sexes, and grades of crimes, totally separated?

7. Are prisoners allowed to see or hold intercourse with each other?

8. Are locks, doors and cells examined daily, and all imperfections reported?

9. Is the system of sentry such as to prevent all efforts to escape?

10. Are officers, or others, allowed to converse with prisoners, or to permit prisoners to address them on other subjects than those of their immediate wants?

11. Does the construction of the prison favor such a breach of good discipline?

12. Is any one under the chief officer allowed to carry anything to or from any prisoner or cell without his permission in each case?

13. What rules prevent the open receiving or secret acquiring of weapons, drugs, spirituous liquor, objectionable printed matter, or other improper articles, by prisoners?

14. Are the property and clothing of every prisoner taken from him, properly kept, and returned to him on his discharge?

15. Are officers or others allowed to talk with each other while on duty?

16. Is boisterous or improper language allowed at any time in any part of the prison?

17. Is the neatness and good order of halls, cells, kitchens, wash-rooms, bathrooms, etc., etc., thorough and universal?

18. Are all utensils properly used? Describe their proper use.

19. Is the removal of all soil and solid and liquid waste adequate and complete?

20. Is the drainage perfect and the building well ventilated and dry?

21. Is there any evidence of decay — especially of decaying wood?

22. Are the sleeping accommodations sufficient and the bedding frequently aired and otherwise thoroughly taken care of?

23. Are the officers obliged to keep a check upon, and report all delinquencies in, the fulfillment of contracts for supplies, etc., as to quantity and quality?

24. Are officers required to report promptly to the physicians all complaints of sickness?

25. Does the physician visit the prison at least once a day and personally examine every prisoner complaining of sickness or reported ill?

26. Does he repair at once to the prison when sent for?

27. Does any other person prescribe medicine to prisoners?

28. Are all drugs in charge of a competent and trustworthy apothecary?

29. Does the physician keep a hospital record?

30. Does he in all cases examine the prisoner after his punishment in solitary, and daily during such confinement, and keep a record of such examinations?

31. Is the diet, clothing and accommodations for the sick, equal to those of hospitals outside of prisons?

32. To whose power and discretion is the discipline of the prison left, and how is he held accountable for abuses?

A great point in such investigations is, wherever a matter is properly the subject of criticism to find out distinctly who is or are responsible for the fault or omission. And another is never to report that anything objectionable cannot be prevented. It can!

These points of inquiry are almost all such as are overlooked by grand juries, etc., in their tours of inspection. The list is incomplete and hastily thrown together. A prison may have all the merits implied in them and still not be a model prison. There is probably not a single one of them to which an investigator of our New Orleans prisons would answer favorably. When half of them can be so answered the community, and not merely the Prison and Asylum Aid Association or the Board of Prison and Asylum Commissioners, will cry "reform it altogether."

PRISON AND ASYLUM REFORM:
A FINAL STATEMENT

[From the New Orleans *Times-Democrat,* March 12, 1882.]

The preliminary work of this enterprise is done. The foundations of a reform of our public institutions were completed on Tuesday evening last, by the organization of the auxiliary association, whose projected office is to aid and hasten the work placed officially in the hands of the Board of Prison and Asylum Commissioners. The board, the ordinance creating the board, and the association, form together the complete machinery of the scheme of reform. Nothing is left now but for the work to move on with fresh and vigorous impulse. It is but just, at this point, to say that the consummation of these important preliminaries, is largely due to the intelligent and liberal enterprise of the publishers of this newspaper.

The work was taken hold of by them, of course, as a pecuniary venture, with the conviction that it would pay. But that is one aspect of the question in which every citizen of New Orleans ought to regard it. It will pay.

It is true that these reforms are a work of humanity and that many have pledged themselves to it with no other idea. But there is another and a perfectly legitimate idea — self-protection. Legititimate, for humanity exercised by society is self-protection, and no self-protection of society is complete, or honorable, without it.

Danger, loss, inhumanity — such are the three conditions that offer themselves as an alternative to the proposed reforms. And it is a conviction not to be despised for its selfish side, that we can no longer *afford* the culpable ignorance and supine negligence which have thus far held back reform.

What has been recognized in these articles and in the promoters of them, and what is now plain to our prison commission and to all the friends of reform, is that the first desideratum is education to the work. The spirit of humanity, the spirit of reform, has never been wholly wanting among us. For a quarter of a century much well-meant preaching and praying and tract distributing has been done in our prisons and municipal asylums. But there they stand! Neither practical, well-informed humanity nor even-handed justice has ever crossed the threshold of one of them; and sentimentality still reigns in our jury-boxes and brutality in our jails.

Now a new leaf is turned. Henceforward the papers of this series will be only the reports of men and women who, after study and investigation, patient and thorough, announce what is, and what ought to be, the state of affairs, or better still, the record of changes actually effected in the interest of humanity and to the advantage of society.

The success of other communities who have revolutionized systems no better than ours forces irresistibly upon us the conviction — the knowledge — that we are killing, where we might be curing, hundreds of insane; that we are confirming, where we might be reforming, hundreds of criminals; and that these operations can be reversed. It is proposed to reverse them.

It is not proposed to dispense with the punishment of crime, but to induce its skillful administration, to eliminate all debasing qualities from it, and to make it in its severest aspects, as well as in its gentler, reformatory and effective.

The present writer passed through a prison last summer where everything indicated a discipline far more rigorous than that of our parish — Inferno; yet such is its effectiveness that it is given as a statistically proven fact that 60 per cent of its inmates never again appear on criminal records.

Under the same administration there is a system of recommending to the criminal courts the cases of such prisoners, generally first offenders, as may be reasonably expected to reform, without punishment. Such are put upon a certain probation within proper restrictions. From October 21, 1878, to December 31, 1879, only 2 per cent of all arraignments were so put upon probation; but of that 2 per cent, which comprised some 536 persons, 87 per cent (say seven out of every eight) have done well.

Such are the results to be sought by the Prisons and Asylums Aid Association of our city. With the motives of the individual member the community need have little to do. The result is all. One may consider public safety; another, public morals; another, religion; but under either standard, the proposal is that everything — whether it be punishment, confinement or treatment — shall be done according to the best art of caring for, and curing, the mentally and morally disordered.

G. W. Cable

The following persons, at the present writing, compose the membership of the association: President, Wm. R. Lyman; vice-presidents, Adolph Schreiber, Edgard Larue, J. P. Davidson, M. D.; treasurer, B. F. Echleman; additional members of the executive committee, Rev. J. H. Nall, D. D., Perry Nugent, Wm. Hartwell and D. C. Holliday, M. D.; secretary, George W. Cable; private members: Rev. Hugh M. Thompson, D. D. [and other names, making a total of nearly 250].